Praise for *The Cauldron and the Drum*

"For practitioners journeying along the path of Celtic shamanism, *The Cauldron and the Drum* is the road map you shouldn't leave home without. With great warmth and compassion, Rhonda McCrimmon teaches readers how to rekindle the spark of magic within their own lives, weave the old ways into the modern day, and achieve personal transformation and healing through time-honored practices."

—Celeste Larsen, author of *Heal the Witch Wound: Reclaim Your Magic and Step into Your Power*

"What Rhonda McCrimmon teaches in this book is nothing short of revolutionary: although we live in a vastly different world than the one our ancestors inhabited, our ability to connect with the divine remains intact . . . . Rhonda shows us how we can develop our spiritual lives while becoming kinder, more grounded, and a better friend to all whom we encounter—including ourselves."

—HeatherAsh Amara, author of the *Warrior Goddess Training* series

"The three cauldrons of energy from the Celtic tradition is a powerful practice that can reap great benefits for anyone walking the shamanic path. Whether you are new to shamanism or Celtic shamanism, Rhonda McCrimmon's *The Cauldron and the Drum* will lead you on the path to shamanic healing."

—Jaime Meyer, president of the Society for
Shamanic Practice, author of *Drumming the Soul
Awake* and *Healing with Shamanism*

"The Celtic mysteries are a spiritual path with many rich threads of wisdom. Rhonda McCrimmon's *The Cauldron and the Drum* is a friendly and accessible introductory guide to the shamanic aspects of this tradition. Her warmth and welcome shine from every page."

—Danú Forest, author of *Wild Magic: Celtic Folk
Traditions for the Solitary Practitioner*

THE
CAULDRON
AND THE
DRUM

THE CAULDRON AND THE DRUM

A JOURNEY INTO CELTIC SHAMANISM

RHONDA McCRIMMON

FOREWORD BY HEATHERASH AMARA
AUTHOR OF THE *WARRIOR GODDESS TRAINING* SERIES

Hierophantpublishing

Cover design by Adrian Morgan
Cover art by Adobe Stock and Shutterstock
Print book interior design by Frame25 Productions

Hierophant Publishing
San Antonio, TX
www.hierophantpublishing.com

If you are unable to order this book from your local
bookseller, you may order directly from the publisher.

Library of Congress Control Number: 2023945512
ISBN: 9781950253456

10 9 8 7 6 5 4 3 2 1

To Scott, for all the things, to my ever-present
Guides, and to the Pod for holding space.

Three candles that illuminate every darkness:
truth, nature, knowledge.
—Ancient Irish Triad

Contents

Foreword

Have you ever taken a moment to consider the fact that, though you might live in a bustling city with all the riches of civilization at your disposal, you undoubtedly have distant ancestors whose lives were deeply intertwined with the land? These ancestors may have foraged for medicines and other resources in the forest, grown and hunted their own food, and paid close attention to the phases of the moon, the cycles of the seasons, and the migrations of birds and other animals. Their emotional and spiritual lives would have been closely tied to the workings of nature, as surely as their physical survival. Shamanic practices such as making offerings at sacred sites and meditating to develop one's intuition would have been commonplace.

What Rhonda McCrimmon teaches in this book is nothing short of revolutionary. Although we live in a vastly different world than the one our ancestors inhabited, our ability to connect with the divine remains intact. We may be surrounded by skyscrapers instead of standing stones, and hear the whir of freeways more often than the sighing of forests, but by intentionally cultivating a sense of reverence and receptivity, we can connect with the spirit of nature and our own inner wisdom.

In my work as the author of the *Warrior Goddess Training* series and as a shamanic teacher, I've seen how much suffering people can experience as a result of disconnection from nature. In the absence of a sense of ourselves being part of a living, breathing web of life, we start to feel lost and alone. We look for meaning in external goals, racking up achievements and collecting possessions, not realizing that it's the simple pleasures of friendship, community, and fully inhabiting our five senses that really make life worth living. *The Cauldron and the Drum* lays out a path that values connection, healing, and celebration above empty striving, and reverence for the natural world that draws us into juicy, living relationships with everything around us.

In my mind, Rhonda McCrimmon is the ultimate warrior goddess, breaking down the real and imaginary barriers that separate us from our divine birthright, and showing us how to carefully and lovingly replenish our inner cauldrons so that we can carry out our souls' work in this world with courage and vigor. Her emphasis on ethical shamanic practice shows us how we can develop our spiritual lives while becoming kinder, more grounded, and better friends to all we encounter—including ourselves.

She also shares the beautiful message that shamanic practices really are for everyone. No matter your gender, race, sexual orientation, or neurotype (McCrimmon herself has ADHD), shamanism can help you tap into your higher self and shed the fears and hesitations that have been holding you back. By following the example of the ancient Celts and putting humility, reverence, and honesty at the center of your spiritual practice, your life will become richer and more joyous—your cauldrons full and your drumbeat steady.

I'm so excited for you to read this book—I know you're going to enjoy it just as much as I did.

Sincerely,
HeatherAsh Amara

The Shaman's Path

Have you ever had the sense that something ancient and vital was missing from your life? Have you felt a twinge of sadness after listening to a piece of folk music or reading a fairy tale, wishing that your days, too, could be charged with magic?

Perhaps you've had an inkling that there is more to reality than meets the eye—something that can't be measured on a scale or poured in a test tube. Maybe these feelings grow especially strong when you gaze up at a grove of trees, when you stand at the edge of a mist-covered lake, when you read a poem, or when you listen to the timeless rhythm of a drum.

If so, you are not alone. Like many ancient peoples, the Celts believed that the visible world was only one layer of a complex and multifaceted reality. In addition to the everyday labor required to put food on the table and keep a roof over their heads, the Celts practiced extensive inner work, honoring the mysteries of their own psyches and seeking the wisdom within. They were also careful to maintain their relationships with the world of nature, knowing that all energy comes from—and returns to— the earth. By making offerings, conducting rituals, and practicing various kinds of meditation, the ancient Celts developed their spiritual gifts and manifested their creative potential.

Today, Celtic shamans are carrying on these ancient traditions: exploring the unconscious mind, connecting with the divine inspiration of the bards, and forging relationships with the land and any spirits who may dwell therein. Celtic shamanism invites us to peer through the mist that divides our "ordinary" mind from our deepest depths. It teaches us to cultivate our inner wisdom and transcend our limited egos to realize our true nature as beings of infinite love. It puts us in touch with the ancient energies of the oak tree, the deer, the bonfire, and the moon— energies which have been drowned out by the clamor of modern technology but are just waiting for us to rediscover them.

Walking a shaman's path means embracing the best of what the ancient world had to offer, while celebrating the myriad possibilities available to us in our own time. It means recognizing that no matter where you live or what type of society you were born into, the basic elements of life remain unchanged. We all live under the same sun, drink the same water, and breathe the same air as our ancestors did hundreds or thousands of years ago. We all need to tend our relationships with the earth, with each other, and with ourselves; we all need meaning, purpose, and community. Each of us has the potential to transform ourselves, using the same tools that have been available to humanity since the first shamans walked the earth— and perhaps to discover some new ones as well.

Indigenous shamans are considered healers of their communities. Using the practices in this book, you can become your own healer—and call yourself a Celtic shaman if that language appeals to you. At the same time, you don't have to call yourself a shaman to receive the benefits of living a shamanic way of life. Those benefits will come when you do the practices that I describe in this book.

My Story

Although I was born and raised in Scotland, I grew up with little understanding of the pre-Christian spiritual traditions of northern Europe. As a teen and twentysomething, I tried on different spiritual practices the way some people try on diets, searching for a path in which my soul felt at home. I spent some time connecting with Christianity; then it was Buddhism and zazen; then Krishnamurti and the religion of no-religion; then Toltec shamanism with its emphasis on personal freedom.

I benefited tremendously from the wisdom of these lineages—but I was also deeply curious about the spiritual traditions rooted in the lands in which I lived. While I could be inspired by stories of Quetzalcoatl and Lord Krishna, and fervently agreed with many of the principles they embodied, these traditions never quite felt like home to me. I was a Scottish woman more familiar with misty hillsides than dusty pyramids, oats and honey than *kulfi*, and Arthurian legends than koans. Where were the spiritual practices native to the Celtic lands I inhabited? And why, when I went to my favorite bookstores in Edinburgh or Glasgow, could I find shelves of books about the religions of Japan, Pakistan, and Israel, but almost none about the spiritual practices of pre-Christian Europe?

Spiritual practices don't emerge in a vacuum. They are tied to the lands in which they first developed. Catholic churches around the world import palm leaves for Palm Sunday whether or not they are anywhere near a palm grove. Some Native American ceremonies involve burning white sage, which only grows in a small area of California. Even though these practices evolved and adapted as they spread far from their point of origin, there are always threads tying them back to their home place.

I wanted to follow a thread which brought me back to the lakes, hills, and moors of Scotland—to its stony outcroppings and hidden caves, its springs and meadows and streams. To its songs and stories and artwork, its tastes and smells, its plants and animals, and the practices of its native people. With all due respect to the wisdom and sacredness of other traditions, I was deeply curious about how my own ancestors might have engaged with the sacred. My research led me to Celtic shamanism (also called Seership in Scotland), a tradition that was suppressed by Christian conquerors, just like so many other spiritual traditions around the world.

Not only did I discover wonderful similarities between the traditions of the ancient Celts and those of the Buddhists, yogis, and dervishes whose philosophies I'd spent years absorbing, but I also found some unique differences that delighted and inspired me. I'll be explaining those in more detail throughout this book.

How to Use This Book

I have written the book I craved at the beginning of my path: a clear and practical guide to nature-based shamanism rooted in Celtic lands, with a focus on living a fulfilling life. As the title of the book suggests, I have organized the material around two central themes: the cauldron and the drum.

The ancient Celts believed in three energy centers in the human body, known as the three cauldrons. By tending and nourishing these three cauldrons, a shaman could receive clear guidance from her intuition, put her insights into practice effectively, and overcome the internal barriers of ego and self-delusion. Throughout these pages, I will take you on a journey from the lowest cauldron to the highest one, sharing practices to cultivate each cauldron's unique potential. Each chapter will contain several exercises designed to activate and balance your inner cauldrons, while giving you the tools you need to effect deep personal transformation. I recommend getting a journal before you begin, as several of these exercises involve self-reflection.

Just like making any other significant change in your life, working with your three cauldrons can shake things up a little, especially at the start. You may go through phases where you feel more emotional than usual, or have unexpected spikes or dips in your energy level. You may need more time alone—or feel an even greater need to connect with others. If you work slowly and carefully, using the exercises in this book, these experiences should remain firmly within the realm of challenging-but-manageable. If you find yourself becoming overwhelmed, slow down or take a break. The cauldron and the drum aren't going anywhere, and are always available to you when you have the time and strength to return to them. No matter how much or how little you engage in shamanic practice, know that your life is already sacred. You are already embraced in the web of life: perfect, secure, and complete.

Chapter 1

Celtic Shamanism Then and Now

The Celts were a group of ancient peoples who lived in an area stretching from Britain to the Black Sea—in other words, a large part of what is now known as Europe. A fierce, wise, and deeply spiritual people, they were revered for their metal-working, their music, and the uncanny abilities of their seers and druids—or, to use a word more commonly known today, their shamans.

In the ancient world, of course, shamanism wasn't a fringe activity practiced by very few, but a common spiritual practice. If you asked an everyday Celt (or, for that matter, an everyday Viking, Toltec, or Navajo) whether their local mountain was sacred, or whether finding and following your intuition was important, or whether leading a life of honesty and goodwill toward others was necessary for happiness, they would have laughed: *Of course! What kind of fool would even have to ask?* In Europe, it was only with the arrival of the Roman Empire and Christianity that the magic of stones, lakes, and winds was silenced and the art of following your inner authority was forgotten, all replaced by a distant god in the sky and a handful of cloaked men who claimed to be his only true spokesmen.

Many of us now associate the word *shamanism* with either South American peoples such as the Quechua or with North American Native groups. Although there is some debate over the etymology of the word, *shamanism* has come to refer to the spiritual practices of native peoples around the world prior to the formation of organized religion.

A close look at the history of human spiritual traditions reveals that what we now call shamanism was once practiced by people on every continent. So it doesn't matter if your eyes are blue or brown, or whether you grew up in Nova Scotia or New Mexico—some of your ancestors most likely practiced what we would now call shamanism. And so did everybody else's!

Like other shamanic traditions around the world, Celtic shamanism was, and is, nature-based, emphasizing the cycle of the seasons, drawing inspiration from plants and animals, and incorporating natural features of the landscape into ceremonies, rituals, and meditations. Celtic shamanism is also self-reflective, with a strong focus on cultivating the inner world of the mind and emotions. This is made evident by the Celts' emphasis on the three cauldron power centers, which we will explore in detail over the course of this book.

Of course, the emphasis on self-reflection isn't surprising. Virtually every ancient spiritual tradition teaches the importance of cultivating the inner qualities of love, honesty, forgiveness, and personal responsibility. You can see this in the ancient writings of the Indian Vedas and the Buddhist Sutras, the oral traditions of North and South American Native peoples and of the ancient Greeks, and many others.

The Celts were an oral culture, passing their history and traditions down through story. The resultant lack of written records means that most of what we know about them has been extrapolated from archeological findings, from the writings of the Romans who conquered them, and from the songs, stories, and myths that have been passed down to this day.

Due to the absence of written records, we are missing many specific details about how the ancient Celts carried out their spiritual practices. We have no step-by-step instructions for their rituals, or encyclopedias of commentary on the exact meanings of their symbols. This frustrating lack of information isn't limited to Celtic shamanism. Anyone studying Celtic *anything*—whether that's music, agriculture, or shamanism—has to rely on what they can glean from the written accounts of other ancient peoples who encountered the Celts. These ancient authors—many of them Roman—were often heavily influenced by Christianity, and were not inclined to record the details of "pagan" practices even if they had been privy to them.

The good news is that spiritual practice is not historical reenactment, and neither is this book! We are not here to obsessively recreate the details of the ancient past, but to discover what shamanism can do for us right here, right now, in *this* world. Just as a modern Christian mass looks quite different from anything that happened in Jesus's time, modern Celtic shamanism draws on the themes of reciprocity, impeccability, and reverence for nature carried down to us from the ancient Celts, while allowing space for the contemporary shaman's own creativity and insight.

Throughout this book, I'll draw on what is factually known about Celtic spiritual practice, while acknowledging instances of extrapolation, imagination, and inspiration. I'll share the practices and rituals which have been transformative in my own life and the lives of my students and clients. Spiritual wisdom is not a matter of birthright or geographic origin, but is available to all of us if we are ready to look within and do the work of cultivating it.

Celtic Shamanism Today

In my view, part of the work of Celtic shamanism today is to reanimate the world—to reverse the cultural trends that numb us to the humming, buzzing, burrowing forms of life that surround us. In this sense, shamanism is an act of deep and radical remembering. When we journey with a drum, leave an offering at the base of a tree, or sit by a river and feed the birds, we are actively invoking our connection to nonhuman forms of life and asserting that we are living beings in a vast and sacred web.

I also want to warn you that practicing Celtic shamanism, or shamanism in any form, is a rebellious act, because in doing so you are reclaiming your own direct connection with the divine—no permission from an expert, authority figure, or guru required. You may also find yourself breaking many of the spoken and unspoken rules with which you grew up—generational patterns which tell you that numbers on a screen are more important than clouds in the sky, that the words in a book are more real than the earth under your feet, and that human beings should converse only with each other, and not with the animals, plants, and unseen beings that surround us all the time.

Next, although Celtic shamanism has its origins in northern Europe, you do not need Celtic heritage in order to benefit from this tradition any more than you need Indian heritage in order to benefit from practicing yoga. Perhaps you are drawn to Celtic shamanism because, like me, your ancestry ties you to these lands—but perhaps your soul resonates with Celtic songs, stories, and rituals even if you come from a different cultural heritage altogether. I want to emphasize that you do not need to have a last name like O'Brien or MacDonald, or a grand-mother in Lochcarron, in order to practice Celtic shamanism. If you are drawn to Celtic practices, this path is open to you.

So what does a Celtic shaman *do*, exactly? And what does it mean to practice in this tradition? Although a hundred different Celtic shamans may have a hundred different answers to these questions, most of them would touch on the following central themes:

Reverence for nature: A Celtic shaman pays close attention to the cycle of the seasons, to the waxing and waning of the moon, to the birds, butterflies, and other creatures in her environment, and to the natural features of her landscape. To a shaman, the natural world is not just background scenery or decoration, but a living, breathing web of life that requires our full participation, and rewards that participation with gifts of insight, healing, and belonging.

Ethics: In a well-known response to St. Patrick, the Irish bard Oisin spoke of what sustained his people before Christianity came to Ireland:

> *The truth of our hearts*
> *The strength of our arms*
> *And the constancy of our tongues.*

Now, as in Oisin's time, Celtic shamanism emphasizes the values of honesty, humility, and reverence—both in spiritual practice and in everyday life. By living these values, you can ground deeply into your authentic self and become an example of strength, kindness, and courage for others.

Respect for the spoken word: The ancient Celts had a special reverence for the power of the spoken word, and took great care with how they used it. Poets were highly esteemed for their artful use of language, which the Celts saw as a gift from the gods, something uniquely human and unmatched by any other animal in the natural world. In modern Celtic shamanism, we pay careful attention to how we speak to others and to ourselves, because we understand the power of the word. Some practitioners also use their word to create beautiful spoken or sung invocations—for example, while opening and closing space, setting an intention, or conducting healing rituals.

Shamanic journeying: Like other shamanic traditions around the world, many Celtic shamans (myself included!) practice a form of trance journeying to gain healing and insight from the depths of their subconscious. By sitting with a drum and focusing deeply on your intention while letting go of your ordinary thought processes, you can allow your inner wisdom to bubble up in unexpected forms, including images, sounds, physical sensations, and subtle inner knowings. Shamanic journeying is popular among practitioners who enjoy a more active style of meditation, and has much in common with creative visualization and other techniques that harness the incredible power of the imagination.

Healing: Shamans have long been called upon to aid those suffering from illness of all kinds—physical, emotional, mental, and spiritual. Some Celtic shamans practice a form of energy healing in which they bridge the distance between this world and the Otherworld, allowing benevolent spirits to remove an unwelcome force from their own or another person's body—for example, unraveling a knot representing a relationship with an ex-partner, or sweeping away the dust and gunk of a long depression. These experiences can be very meaningful to the people involved and often result in real feelings of relief. Although some highly trained and experienced shamans do offer healing services to others, the most important healing work is that which we do for ourselves. In Celtic shamanism, we are continuously peeling away the layers of our own defenses, uncovering the deep wells of love that lie beneath them. We gently examine our own minds to see where they are ruled by fear, and work slowly and carefully to release this fear. By doing this courageous work, we train ourselves to act with intention and integrity in all situations, and bring our highest selves to all of our relationships—both with other humans and with the natural world.

Personal transformation: Shamanism is a path of both internal and external transformation. By looking within, and meeting what we find with love and kindness, we allow ourselves to grow. Sometimes, this growth can be uncomfortable. It can mean facing old fears and forgiving ourselves or others for the wounds of the past—but the rewards are wisdom, clarity, and unconditional love. At the same time, Celtic shamanism leads us on a path of external transformation, changing the way we relate to the natural world and the actions we take or refrain from taking in all our relationships. In other words, its power lies not only in healing our past but in opening a new way of being in the future. The Celts knew that change is a potent force, and this is just as true today as it always was.

An Evolving Tradition

If you choose to walk this path, know that your shamanic practice will not look the same as mine or anyone else's—and that's a good thing! While we are all connected, we are also all unique. As a living, growing, evolving tradition, Celtic shamanism invites us to simultaneously explore our sameness and our diversity. With this in mind, you may find that some of the practices I suggest don't speak to you, and that's okay. If a particular exercise doesn't appeal to or resonate with you, I invite you to either discard it or—better yet—experiment with changing it into something that could work for you. As you practice, remember that it's your intentions that matter the most.

In the modern world, we often expect everything to be codified, with detailed instruction manuals and guidelines to follow. While this works well for many things, it's not necessarily the best approach when it comes to spiritual practice. A spiritual practice that engages the mind, body, and imagination will nourish you far more than a practice based on blind rule-following. For this reason, shamanism has always been creative, flexible, and open to interpretation.

Celtic shamanism has the power to transform you at a deep level, changing the way you relate to life and allowing you to grow in ways you never imagined. But shamanism isn't only about personal growth. The gifts you cultivate through your shamanic work are urgently needed by the people, plants, and animals all around you. The earth is in crisis. Not only are we losing species at a rapid pace, but human suffering is increasing in the face of climate change, economic insecurity, and cultural and political divisions. By working with the practices in this book, you can uncover the inner strength and clarity that will make you a powerful agent of change—a protector of the planet, an ally to your fellow humans, and a friend to the plants and animals who also call this place home.

Chapter 2

Tools of Transformation

Of all the cherished objects in my home, there are two I hold most dear. The first is a small black cauldron that lives on the shelf beside my kitchen stove, and the second is the frame drum that hangs on the wall in the upstairs room I use for shamanic journeying. Like thousands of shamans who walked the hills of northern and central Europe before me, I use these objects in my spiritual practice every day. My drum transports me across the thin veil that hangs between ordinary consciousness and the depths of my psyche; and my cauldron grounds and nourishes me, reminding me to tend my energy just as carefully as I would tend a simmering stew.

The cauldron recurs frequently in Celtic folklore, myth, and poetry as a symbol of transformation. Although the humble cauldron was used by Celts to cook their daily porridge, cauldrons were also understood to be power objects. Wealthy chiefs and warlords often possessed huge cauldrons made out of precious metals, with intricate designs stamped into their sides. Large, ornate cauldrons were not only a status symbol among Celtic peoples; they were also thought to have magical properties. For example, the Celts believed that drinking mead from such a cauldron on the eve of battle could transform ordinary men into immortal warriors.

One Celtic myth tells of the Cauldron of Dagda, one of the four treasures the Tuatha Dé Danann brought to Ireland from the Otherworld. The Cauldron of Dagda was a magical vessel said to provide an endless supply of food to those who possessed it—an important asset at a time when the reach of a chieftain's power was defined by his ability to feed an army.

In another tale, the Welsh goddess Cerridwen possessed a magical cauldron said to grant wisdom and knowledge to those who drank from it. One day, Cerridwen brewed a potion to give to her son, and put a young boy named Gwion Bach in charge of guarding the cauldron as it cooked. Three drops of the brew accidentally fell on the boy's finger, and he was suddenly filled with the knowledge and power the potion held. Cerridwen chased Gwion for many months until she finally caught him. She swallowed him, and nine months later she gave birth to Taliesin, the greatest of all Welsh poets.

Cauldrons boil and bubble, transforming base ingredients into powerful potions, and tough, inedible grains into nourishing food. Tending a cauldron requires patience and alertness; fall asleep, and you can end up with a sticky, burned mess instead of the medicine you were intending. It also requires a certain amount of grace: treat your cauldron roughly, and you can knock it right off the fire, spilling the precious substance within. Finally, as Cerridwen's story shows, there are perils to entrusting the care of your cauldron to another—this is work best done by and for yourself.

The Three Cauldron Energy Centers

Since ancient times, sages and mystics around the world have perceived the existence of energy centers within the human body: specific points, typically found along the spine, which are associated with different aspects of our physical, emotional, and spiritual functioning. These energy centers have been given different names by various cultural and spiritual groups, and been described in different ways. For example, the yogis of India called these energy centers *chakras*, and identified seven located between the crown of the skull and the tailbone. The sages of China described three *dantien* whose energy could be cultivated and circulated through practices like tai chi and Qigong for optimal physical and emotional health. Some North American Native tribes conceived of energy centers through which the soul entered the body.

The ancient Celts believed in three inner cauldrons responsible for storing and cultivating energy within every human being. The eighth century bard Amergin Glúingel wrote of these cauldrons in his famous poem *The Cauldron of Poesy,* which describes each cauldron's qualities in detail. The Celts believed that when all three of these cauldrons are working harmoniously, a person gains access to their full potential. When your three cauldrons are in balance, you're at peace with yourself and the world around you, and you're more likely to be in optimal physical, mental, emotional, and spiritual health. When they're out of balance, you can suffer from things like physical exhaustion, confusion and indecision, anxiety, low self-worth, and fear. You may also become highly reactive, having emotional outbursts whose root causes you don't understand, and find yourself in patterns of conflict with others.

The lower cauldron, known as *coire goriath*, or the cauldron of warming, has strong parallels with the root chakra in the Indian framework. It is the site of grounding and connection, belonging, and trust. Just as an acorn contains all the fat and nutrients required to launch an oak tree into the world, *coire goriath* contains the energy you need to accomplish your purpose in life. Unfortunately, this cauldron can get tipped over by adverse experiences in childhood such as trauma or neglect, allowing this precious life fuel to run low. Being disconnected from nature can also deplete this life force energy from the lower cauldron—something that is especially common in our fast-paced technological world. If you've ever felt like you're "running on empty," a tipped-over lower cauldron could be the culprit.

The rewards of righting and filling your lower cauldron are legion. You will gain access to stores of energy that were previously inaccessible to you— energy which can be used to power all aspects of your life. When your lower cauldron is upright and full, your career, relationships, artistic pursuits, and spiritual practice can all thrive, because they have the necessary fuel. Think of the way that flowers and vegetables can grow big and healthy when the soil is rich in organic matter, versus when the soil is dry and depleted. Your lower cauldron is the "soil" of your life, and tending it allows everything you plant to grow and flourish.

The middle cauldron, known as *coire erma*, or the cauldron of motion, shares some features with the Indian heart chakra. This cauldron is responsible for your sense of compassion, forgiveness, and love—both for yourself and for others. It is also the home of your shadow—that collection of wounds that need to be healed in order for you to stay emotionally balanced during challenging times. By tending to this cauldron, you restore your innate ability to live and work from a place of unconditional love. If you've ever felt overwhelmed by the energy of the people around you, and unable to maintain appropriate physical, emotional, or spiritual boundaries, this cauldron is probably out of balance.

The middle cauldron is also known as the cauldron of vocation. This cauldron helps you identify and carry out your soul's purpose on this earth, even in the face of fears and obstacles. A balanced middle cauldron unlocks your ability to serve others and the planet, whether that's through your physical labor, your creative or intellectual gifts, or your kind and compassionate heart. Reorienting your life toward your soul's purpose makes for a joyful existence, even as you continue to experience and learn from the normal griefs, jealousies, and sacrifices of a human life.

The highest cauldron, known as *coire sois*, or the cauldron of wisdom, parallels the Indian crown chakra. It is home to your higher self, and is the portal through which you can receive what the Celts called *imbas forosnai*, or divine wisdom. By working with this cauldron, *imbas forosnai* will appear in the form of intuition, inspiration, and spiritual gifts. If you're feeling uninspired, burned out creatively, or unable to connect with a sense of the divine—or if you frequently find yourself confusing your own ego for divine inspiration—this cauldron could use some tending.

Because the upper cauldron is our portal to intense spiritual energies, working with it requires caution, forbearance, and a sound ethical foundation. Upper cauldron energy can sometimes feed our ego in unhealthy ways, leading us to think that we know what's best for others. Consequently, it's important to temper our egos with humility, reverence, service, and other virtues. By establishing ourselves in virtuous thought and action, we can ensure that our shamanic work will benefit all beings while harming none.

When the upper cauldron is in balance, you feel connected to the divine and present in the moment. You can perceive the sacred in sorrowful moments as well as in joyful ones, and keep your balance during both categories of experience. This quality of steadiness is a sign of spiritual mastery. Balancing your upper cauldron can make you a better friend and more effective mentor, an all-around resource for your community. The benefits of balancing your upper cauldron also trickle back down to your two lower cauldrons, as a calm and equanimous mind is well-equipped to support a strong heart and healthy body.

Throughout the rest of this book, we'll work through these three cauldrons in order from lowest to highest, exploring their deeper meanings and looking at ways to balance them. Cauldron work is raw and juicy. It can put you in touch with your deepest fears and insecurities, while simultaneously unlocking your greatest potential. As your three cauldrons come into harmonious balance, you will find that you feel more connected to yourself, others, and the natural world. You may also begin to feel more grounded, happier, and in tune with a higher intelligence.

When I started my shamanic practice, all three of my cauldrons were in complete disarray. My lowest cauldron was tipped over and leaking, the result of childhood trauma that had left me fearful and ungrounded. My middle cauldron was likewise stuck in a tipped over position, resulting in poor boundaries, a fear of intimacy, and a woeful lack of self-love. As for my highest cauldron—well, let's just say that what I took for spiritual wisdom was no more than the machinations of my ego, and it was humbling to realize that, far from being upright and overflowing with inspiration, this cauldron was upside down.

Now, I check in with my inner cauldrons on a daily basis, paying close attention to the state of each one. Are they empty, simmering nicely, or boiling over? Has the fire beneath them gone out, or perhaps gotten too hot? Does something need to be added or taken out? As for the cauldron in my kitchen, I use it almost every day as well, feeling a powerful thread of connection to my Celtic ancestors whenever I fill it with grain or greens and put it on the fire.

EXERCISE
Saining

Sain means "to bless, consecrate, or make sacred." The practice is Celtic in origin, and is still widely done today. Saining can take many forms, but they all share the intention of imbuing sacredness into a person, place, or object. Sprinkling yourself with water can be a form of saining, as can lighting a candle and watching the flame burn down. In Scotland, some families still sain their houses by burning juniper branches until the whole house fills with smoke, driving out any negative energy within. This practice is often compared to smudging rituals performed by many Native American tribes in North America, or the burning of incense in Eastern spiritual traditions. I sain with juniper after hosting shamanic workshops at my home to ensure that any leftover energy is properly cleared.

While some believe that saining is open only to those of Scottish descent, I believe that anyone who feels called to do so can develop their own saining ritual. In this exercise, I will teach you how to perform a saining ritual that can be used to make sacred or cleanse a person, space, or object.

To begin, gather any elements that feel right to you—maybe that's dried herbs or flowers, a candle, a rattle, a jar of water from a special place, or a juniper stick or incense.

Next, take a few breaths and bring your attention into the present moment. Feel your feet connect with the ground and feel a sense of gratitude for the earth that supports you. If you feel so moved, acknowledge and welcome any spirits or ancestors who are helping you in this process. Next, recall your intention to cleanse or make sacred the object of your intention.

Make a cross symbol (note: this is not the Christian cross but rather an X) with your thumb over the person, object, or space you are cleansing while speaking a few words of invocation and blessing. Let these words come to you spontaneously. It's okay to keep it simple and short. For example, you might say, "I ask that this space be made sacred, and that all who enter feel loved, protected, and at ease."

Next, burn the incense, herbs, or candle, sprinkle the water, shake the rattle, or use whatever elements you've gathered in a way that feels purifying to you. Do so consciously, with your attention in the present moment. Envision the object of your intention receiving the blessing of sacredness and purification.

To close the ritual, take a few deep breaths and say a statement or prayer of gratitude (silently or out loud) for the cleansing and sanctity of the object of your intention. Notice any energetic changes you feel in the coming days around the object of your intention as a result of this ritual.

The Drum

Just like the cauldron, the drum is a tool of transformation. Drumming transforms consciousness, smoothing the rough edges of our noisy, chatty minds and sending us into a gentle state of trance. Drums, rattles, and other percussion instruments can be found in shamanic cultures around the world, fulfilling a deep human need to access the quieter, wilder, more intuitive parts of our minds and imaginations.

There is a long history of drum use in Celtic lands, from the Scottish *wecht* and English riddle to the Irish bodhran. Many of these simple drums started out as agriculture tools for winnowing grain or carrying peat, and Celtic villagers used them in a pinch as musical instruments. Celtic warriors were also known to play hypnotic rhythms on their armor in the moments leading up to battle, putting themselves in the "battle trance" required to overcome their elite Roman enemies. Today, most Celtic shamans use frame drums—wide, shallow drums composed of a simple wooden hoop with either leather or a vegan alternative stretched over it.

When I first started out with shamanism, I felt self-conscious about drumming. Who did I think I was, anyway? Surely *I* didn't have the special skills required to initiate a trance state and go on a shamanic journey, skills I imagined to be the province of highly trained individuals belonging to obscure lineages—in other words, *real* shamans. At the time, I was still operating out of the old paradigm, the one in which I viewed shamanism as an esoteric practice rather than the norm for most human beings throughout history. Since then, I've discovered and rediscovered a basic truth: shamanism really is accessible to everyone.

We all take certain skills for granted. Many of us don't give much thought to the fact that we can speak and write, for example, or that we can walk, run, or dance. Yet all of these are incredible gifts that we had to cultivate, and the vast majority of us perform these skills every single day. Shamanic journeying is the same way. As humans, we all have the ability to initiate trance states—most of us have simply never learned how to do so.

I'll never forget the first time I went on my own self-guided shamanic journey. Although I had journeyed before under the guidance of my shamanic teachers, or using pre-recorded drumming tracks, I was a little nervous that I wouldn't achieve the same results by drumming for myself. What if the physical act of drumming distracted me from the journey, or I somehow failed to find the magic rhythm that would sink me into a trance?

Yet when I picked up the beautiful frame drum a friend had gifted me and began to play, I soon found the opposite was true. With each stroke, a warm wave of resonance washed over me, evoking something ancient and deeply comforting. I felt a sense of profound recognition, as if something deep inside me *knew* this sound. The drum's vibration awakened my spiritual and intuitive side, while lulling my thinking, planning mind into a gentle slumber—exactly as my teachers had told me it would.

As I drummed, I found myself journeying to the unseen realms—what the ancient Celts called the Otherworld, and what people today might call the imagination or the psyche. As my mind relaxed, I began to have a vision of myself crossing a misty lake and entering a magical realm. It felt a lot like the day-dreams I had as a child on summer days, when I'd lie beneath a tree and imagine myself going on wonderful adventures. Carried along by the drumbeat, I saw myself visiting a stone tower and meeting the wizard Merlin, an archetype of wisdom. Grabbing my shoulders, he told me to pay close attention to the ripple effects of my every action. I felt that I had gotten in touch with my own inner wisdom, in a way that was sometimes difficult for me to do in the everyday swirl of life.

Since then, I've taken hundreds of shamanic journeys. Drumming is a meditation for me—a way of setting aside my everyday thoughts and concerns, and getting in touch with the deep truths that lie within. Often while I'm drumming, I'll have insights that seem to float into my head from nowhere, as if whispered to me by a helpful friend. In those moments, it feels like my Guides are leading and protecting me. At the same time, I also have a profound sense of being connected to my higher self—that the wise being whispering in my ear is *me*.

Some practitioners of Celtic shamanism work with spirit guides such as power animals or ancestors who they encounter over the course of meditation. For some people, these spirit guides feel just as real, tangible, and autonomous as human friends. Other Celtic shamans view spirit guides as beautiful metaphors for the various aspects of the self—for example, the wise aspect, the loving aspect, the fiery aspect, and so forth.

Regardless of which camp you fall into, the important thing is to listen carefully to the insights you receive while journeying, and to apply them in your daily life—whether or not you believe they come from your higher self or from an "outside" source such as an ancestor or benevolent spirit.

While prerecorded drumming tracks are wonderful tools and can be found easily online, if you decide to choose to drum for yourself, the first step is acquiring a frame drum—a round drum whose width is greater than its depth. You can buy a drum or make one yourself. Put some thought into the type of hide and frame you choose, as these have special significance. Common woods for frame drums include ash, oak, and willow:

Ash: Associated with beauty and the feminine, ash is a wood of prophecy, fate, and destiny.

Oak: A most exalted tree, the oak was venerated by druids and was associated with celestial beings.

Willow: A gentle wood suggesting new beginnings, willow holds space for personal growth and the rewards of a path well walked. This tree is also associated with bees, pollen, and honey.

The hide you choose for your drum will also have cultural significance. Common drum hides used in Celtic lands include boar, deer, and horse:

Boar: In the earliest known Welsh prose stories, known as the Mabinogion, the boar is associated with ferocity, shapeshifting, and the Underworld. In Irish myth, the pig is often sacrificed for feasts and would continuously resurrect to be eaten again. The Irish sea god Manannán had herds of boars who would reappear after being eaten. Another association is of death and destruction—in the Fionn cycle of tales, a fearsome boar called Formael killed fifty men and dogs in one day. The spirit of boar as a drum is a powerful undertaking!

Deer: Associated with wild nature and the forest, deer are shapeshifters known to lead unwitting humans into the Otherworld—often without their consent. They are also associated with supernatural women and wisdom.

Horse: Representing wealth and power, the horse is associated with inner and outer sovereignty. Horses symbolize speed, beauty, journeys, fertility, and sexuality.

Another drum option is choosing a vegan drum made from plastic rather than wood and hide. I have a vegan drum and it is a most precious and sacred instrument—as well as very practical. While skin drums rarely hold up in wet or humid conditions, my vegan drum gives me the privilege of ritual drumming outside in Scotland in any weather. Choose a drum based on your heart's knowing and it will become not only a bridge to the unseen realms but a much-loved friend on your shamanic path.

Celtic Meditation

Virtually all of the world's spiritual traditions include a form of meditation, and Celtic shamanism is no different. Think of drumming as the shamanic equivalent of zazen—a way to deeply observe your inner workings in whatever form they arise. Although Celtic shamanism places less formal emphasis on the breath than some other forms of meditation, you will find that your breath often becomes deeper and more regular when you are drumming. Many people report feeling a sense of peace when they drum, and an accompanying shift into a higher perspective.

Journeying with a drum is not the only way Celtic shamans meditate. Walking in nature, tending a garden, making offerings, writing songs and poetry, and even cooking are all time-honored forms of connecting with the divine. By doing these things consciously and with reverence, we connect to the best parts of being human, and remind ourselves of why we're alive.

The Importance of Awareness

No matter how you choose to explore your inner landscape, you'll need to cultivate awareness to do it well. The word *awareness* can mean different things in different traditions, but in this context I'm referring to the quality of attention you bring to your internal and external experiences. For example, how finely can you pay attention to the sounds of the birds when you're walking in nature? How closely can you track your own emotions as they arise and dissipate? Can you saturate these experiences with love and acceptance as they are happening?

Think of awareness as the broth in which your consciousness is steeping. When you steep your mind in the qualities of lightness, alertness, and gentleness, you can navigate even the most uncomfortable experiences with relative ease. This becomes very important when you're undertaking the big transformations that go along with balancing your inner cauldrons. Your cauldron work will go much more smoothly if you can bring consistent, loving attention to everything you are thinking, feeling, and perceiving. Throughout this book, I will share my favorite practices for developing the skill of awareness.

EXERCISE
Building Awareness

Although the word *awareness* can sound like some exalted spiritual state (and it is!), it is actually very simple. Whenever you pay close attention to something—anything—you are being aware. Try this simple exercise to see what I mean.

To start, choose a small object in your home. It could be a shoe, a dish, a flower, or anything else within arm's reach.

Pretend that you are seeing this object for the first time. Remember that the object's name is just a convention we use for communicating with one another. Take a moment to experience the object beyond its name, as if you are discovering it for the first time. Not only that, but pretend that this is your one chance to examine this object before it disappears forever.

How does your perception change, knowing that this is your only chance to see, feel, and handle this object before it is gone? Do you feel a new-found appreciation for the color and texture of the object, or for its emotional significance? Do you feel that you are literally seeing it more clearly, and with something like greater reverence?

Repeat this exercise whenever you wish to sharpen your attention and enter a heightened state of awareness.

▲▼

Choosing a Path of Transformation

As we continue our journey into Celtic shamanism, I invite you to embrace the magic and symbolism of the cauldron and the drum. By working with these two power objects, whether in a literal or metaphorical sense, you can tap into the ancient wisdom that Celtic peoples have known for centuries: the cauldron and the drum are not mere accessories on the shaman's path, but potent vehicles of transformation.

Use them wisely, and you invite change to occur where it matters most, within your beautiful self.

▲▼▲

EXERCISE
Shamanic Journeying

A basic shamanic journey consists of opening sacred space, setting an intention, initiating a trance state with your Guides, remaining in the trance state for as long as feels fruitful, closing sacred space, and recording your experiences in a journal. Let's take each step one at a time, but first a word of advice: It is important that you have no attachment to the outcome of this ritual. Whether you have a "successful," "productive" journey is not the point; we are simply practicing surrendering into the loving arms of the divine.

Open sacred space by saining, shaking a rattle, burning incense, or making other ritual gestures that feel significant to you. Call on any Guides, ancestors, archetypes, or spirit beings whose qualities you would like to invoke on your journey. Whether or not you know who your Guides are yet, it is important not to undertake a journey alone.

Set your intention by speaking aloud what you wish to achieve on your journey. For example, you might say,

"Show me what I'm not seeing in this situation" or "Show me how I can be a better parent/partner/friend."

Initiate a trance state by playing your drum or a prerecorded drumming track. It can take up to fifteen minutes of steady drumming to enter a trance state, so be patient and make sure you're sitting or lying down in a comfortable position.

Remain in the trance state for as long as it takes for your subconscious to send out messages and symbols related to your intention. You may receive images, sounds, or physical sensations. When you feel complete, allow your drumming to slow down to a halt.

Close sacred space by rattling or burning incense again, and thank any Guides, ancestors, archetypes, or power animals to whom you feel grateful.

Record your impressions in a journal, noting any symbols or verbal messages you received. Brainstorm possible meanings for these impressions, as well as what actions these might suggest for your life.

You may choose to journey as frequently or infrequently as you please. The important thing is to journey with intention and respect, paying careful attention to space opening and closing rituals.

Chapter 3

Filling the Lower Cauldron

I remember walking into a field of flowers when I was a little girl and feeling a sense of awe as the wind made thousands of bright yellow petals nod and sway all around me. The earth was warm and crumbly under my feet, and I could see fuzzy black bees roaming from flower to flower, pollinating each one. It felt like the bees, the flowers, and the earth itself were friends with each other and with me, and we were all doing a beautiful dance together. In that moment, it seemed to me that life was charged with infinite potential, and all I had to do was make a wish and anything my heart desired would be granted to me. I felt supported by the earth under my feet, protected by the blue sky above my head, and surrounded by a loving energy I couldn't quite name.

Twenty years later, I was a stressed single mother working two jobs by day and going to accounting school at night. After growing up in a chaotic household with an alcoholic father and a passive, incapable mother, I'd escaped into the arms of a man who was dealing with childhood trauma of his own. I'd gotten pregnant quickly after we met, but he kicked me and our daughter out in the middle of the night one year after she was born. Now, it took all the energy I had just to scrape through each day. Even on the odd night when I did get enough sleep, I still woke up feeling depleted—as if the nourishment flowing into me was draining right back out again.

Now, anyone who's lived with infants or young children understands the deep, exhausting demands of new parenthood. There is a profound level of tiredness that comes with caring for someone around the clock. But even as my daughter grew and turned two, and then three, and then four, my fatigue was showing no signs of letting up. Not only was I exhausted all the time, but I'd seemingly lost my ability to recharge my batteries at all. I hadn't been in a great place before my daughter was born, but her entry really put a fine point on how unsustainable my lifestyle had become. I needed to figure out a better way—not only for myself, but for her, too.

If I'd had the good fortune to visit a Celtic shaman at that moment in my life, I would have learned that I was suffering from a classic case of lower cauldron drain—an extremely common ailment in today's fast-paced modern world. I was trapped in survival mode, cut off from my soul's purpose and from any sense of connection to nature and the divine. Although I was doing what I had to do to ensure my daughter's future, it would take more than an accounting degree to get back on my feet. I needed to find a way to replenish my spiritual and emotional reserves, not just my financial ones.

The ancient Celts believed that the lower cauldron—also known as *coire goriath*, or the cauldron of warming—is upright and full at birth, brimming with the juicy life force that every human needs to make her way from infancy to childhood to adulthood. Just as the Chinese sages speak of chi, the yogis of India speak of prana, and the Toltecs speak of the nagual, Celtic shamanism recognizes the divine energy that exists within each person, as well as each plant, animal, stone, and element of nature. While the exact name the ancient Celts used to describe this life force is lost to history, I use the Gaelic phrase *brìgh na beatha*, which means "substance or essence of life."

As infants, we do not yet possess the skills we need to tend to the *brìgh na beatha* that fills our lower cauldron. We need loving, available parents and role models to protect this cauldron on our behalf until we are old enough to take on that responsibility. Yet all too often, we don't receive the protection we need. Abuse, neglect, or traumatic events in childhood can knock this cauldron off the fire, allowing its precious contents to leak out. Even when our parents were loving and present, virtually no one reaches adulthood without some form of trauma or adverse experience that can deplete our *brìgh na beatha*.

One could argue that merely growing up in a modern industrial society is traumatic, no matter how wonderful your parents were. How many of us have ever had the chance to breathe truly clean air, drink pure water that didn't come from a treatment plant, or get to know the plants, animals, and landforms of our home place? How many of us grew up dancing under the full moon, feeling the warmth of a bonfire on our skin, and listening to the joyous laughter of family and friends? Most of us were raised indoors, with a television or computer for company. This state of chronic disconnection from nature may be a "quiet" form of trauma, but it is deeply damaging nonetheless.

As part of this disconnection from nature, many of us were socialized by our parents, teachers, or the culture at large to believe that acquiring money and material possessions is the ultimate measuring stick of success. Not only that, but we learn that each one of us is responsible for achieving these things on our own in a hypercompetitive world. Instead of growing up in the security of an extended family and community, learning a trade or lifeway passed down through generations, we are pushed into an industrial workforce where we must be productive and efficient at all costs.

Often, our work is completely abstracted from the "real" world, and takes our minds and bodies far away from the living, breathing earth. We learn that our value as human beings is contingent on how well we perform in artificial or abstract environments, then wonder why we feel lost and overwhelmed at the end of the day. Furthermore, since no amount of money or material possessions is ever enough, we can always find ways to judge ourselves harshly, no matter what we do.

As a result, your lower cauldron can become drained by adhering to the false belief that you must achieve some imaginary idea of perfection in order to be worthy of love, or that you must be famous, successful, or otherwise revered by others for your life to have value. These beliefs may be operating far below the level of conscious awareness, but they can steadily eat away at your life force, leaving you in a state of chronic depletion.

The good news is that these false beliefs can change. The more you work with your lower cauldron, the more you will realize that you are loveable and beloved exactly as you are. We are all born perfect and complete. Just as the flowers and trees are beautiful manifestations of nature, so are we—the trick is pushing through the layers of fear and self-judgment that prevent us from seeing it. And just as the flowers and trees draw support from the earth, sun, and rain, we can draw on the power of seen and unseen forces to help us.

EXERCISE
Guardian Guide Visualization

Celtic shamans believe that we each have a protector spirit, similar to a guardian angel—a loving being we can call upon for support and companionship when we're engaged in difficult inner work.

To begin, think of a time when you felt a strong sense of being protected. If you have a hard time calling to mind a specific incident, it's perfectly fine to imagine one. Spend as much time as you need to call those feelings of safety into your body.

Next, imagine yourself in a quiet place, such as a clearing in the forest. Ask your guardian guide to step forward and make him- or herself known to you. Imagine this Guide using as many of your senses as possible. What do they look like? What does their voice sound like? What sensations do you feel in your body when they are near? Does this Guide have a name? Do they have wings, a cape, or a halo?

The next time you feel overwhelmed or fearful, call this Guide into your mind. You can do this by making a verbal or silent request for your Guide to come forward or by visualizing them in as much detail as possible. Once you feel that your Guide is present, allow them to filter out all unwanted energy, allowing only what is for your best and highest good to come through.

No matter where you are, you can always invoke the qualities of love, protection, and courage by using this technique. This can give you the strength to put one foot in front of the other, proceeding with the knowledge that you are already complete.

▲▽

Filling Your Lower Cauldron

The world the ancient Celts inhabited was far more elemental than our own. Every day, they were surrounded by the magic of rippling water, the excitement of a crackling bonfire, and the mysterious whispers of tree branches in the wind. They would have encountered wild animals on a more regular basis than most of us do today—graceful deer and leaping stags, shy hares and ornery sheep, and birds and insects of all descriptions. There was no epidemic of "nature deficiency disorder" to contend with. Living in close alignment with nature was the ordinary state of most people.

This connection with the natural world means that persistent, ongoing lower cauldron drain would have been far less common among the ancient Celts than it is in modern society. Nature is the original cauldron-filler, our original store of life force. And our connection with nature is what keeps our lower cauldrons full long after we've grown into adults. Yet adulthood is exactly the time when many of us find it hardest to get any meaningful time in nature at all, and our paved-over urban environments certainly don't help.

Complicating things even further is the fact that many of us were brought up to believe that nature is something to be looked at from a distance, rather than an extension of our own bodies and consciousnesses. Unlike the ancient Celts, who would have gathered wood, water, herbs, mushrooms, and other resources from their home environments as a matter of course, many of us can't name the trees or plants in our local environments, much less their medicinal, technological, and culinary uses.

When we engage with nature on a deep level—by watching it closely, allowing it to hypnotize, astound, or confuse us, and encouraging our long-buried curiosity to come to life—we begin to transform. Making the intimate acquaintance of a natural place and its nonhuman inhabitants helps you to realize that there's more to life than whatever familiar monologue is running through your head. We are surrounded by other consciousnesses—a fact the ancient Celts knew well, but which most of us moderns have forgotten.

A friend of mine lived on the edge of a big city in what he described as a "cookie-cutter" neighborhood, one with small houses on small lots, placed very close together. Sadly, the first thing the developer did when building the neighborhood was to go in and cut down all the existing trees, including numerous old oaks, because building the roads and houses was easier on a cleared piece of land.

My friend, who longed to deepen his connection to nature, committed to going on a walk in his neighborhood every day. On his very first walk, he discovered a majestic old oak on the edge of the subdivision which somehow had been spared. He approached the tree with the intention of fully noticing and appreciating it. Standing in its shade, he peered up through the branches and marveled at its grandeur. He placed his hands on its massive trunk and felt the energy that it held. He contemplated how this oak was once a tiny acorn that had dropped from a neighboring tree and experienced just the right conditions to germinate. Water. Sun. Carbon dioxide. Nutrients from the soil. The giant that stood before him started as a little acorn, one that was full of life force.

As he returned home, something shifted in him. Suddenly, he saw and felt nature everywhere—even in his neighborhood, which had felt so sterile before. He realized the well-manicured grass was a part of nature. The weeds in the flower beds were nature too. There was also the humming of insects, the chirping of birds, and the croaking of frogs. He also became conscious of the low hills to the east, and the wide, slow-moving river several miles to the west. Even though he couldn't see either of these things right before his eyes, he realized that he was nevertheless connected to them and supported by them.

My friend made nature walks a regular part of his practice and began to leave small offerings at the oak tree as a way of deepening his relationship with that special place. He realized that even in a cookie-cutter neighborhood, the land and its life forms deserved to be loved and honored—indeed, maybe it was even more important to do so in a place that most people didn't see as being alive.

▲▼

EXERCISE
Nature Offerings

If you're not used to spending time in nature and aren't quite sure what to do with yourself when you go outdoors, it can help to have some goal or task to carry out. For example, you might collect pebbles or flowers, keep an eye out for certain birds or animals, or leave an offering at a specific natural site, such as a riverbend, outcropping of stones, or the base of a majestic old tree. The Celts were fond of making offerings to the gods at springs, lakes, and other watery places, which they considered to be doorways to the unseen realms.

Offerings are a core element of my shamanic practice, and I encourage all my students to get into this habit as well. If you feel so moved, you can identify the places which are sacred to the Indigenous people in your area, and you can make offerings there. You can also simply decide that a certain tree, pond, or hillside is sacred to *you*. There's no application process for designating a part of the earth as holy—it is all sacred, after all. Once you have identified your own repertoire of sacred places, make a point to visit them frequently, showing them your appreciation and basking in their beauty.

Why do this? First, there is the idea that giving up something of value—whether it's a spoonful of oats and honey, incense, or a prized piece of jewelry—puts us in relationship with the person, place, or being to whom we are making the offering. When you give a birthday present to a neighbor, you establish a bond—a bond which would take time and effort to develop into a meaningful friendship, but a bond nonetheless. Likewise, when you toss an offering into a lake, you stitch yourself to that place energetically. It becomes a little more part of you, and you become a little more part of it.

Another way of looking at offerings is to see them as an acknowledgment that your consciousness is not entirely *yours*—your life is supported by everything around you, including plants and animals, other humans, and the rest of the natural world. You do not exist in a vacuum. Your life is both a gift *and* dependent on others. Leaving an offering is a way of saying, "Hey, I know I can never fully account for the tremendous gift of life, so whoever and whatever is out there, just know that I'm grateful."

Although it may feel strange at first to "waste" perfectly good items by leaving them out as offerings, I encourage you to try it and see how you feel. The Celts could ill afford to waste the resources of food or the precious metal that went into the swords and jewelry they offered at sacred sites, yet they sacrificed these valuable objects all the same. Making offerings is a way of asserting your dignity and reminding yourself of your own abundance: *I may not have everything, but I can afford to give something.* Not only are you whole and complete, but you have the power to be generous—and this is a tremendous source of strength.

Childhood Review

Once you've established a relationship with nature, I invite you to set aside some time to review your childhood and formative years. The goal of this review is to identify the events that may have knocked your lower cauldron off-balance, and to begin reclaiming your power from them. This type of shamanic recapitulation is taught in different ways by different teachers around the world. The version I teach is designed to be simple and straightforward—a good rule of thumb when it comes to lower cauldron work.

While you can conduct a review of your past at any time, I recommend doing this after a nature walk, because your lower cauldron will get a little bump in life force which will help you through the process. Before I reviewed my own childhood, I first spent a couple of hours walking around a lake near my home.

As I walked, I absorbed the stillness and serenity of the water—qualities which helped me to stay calm and present during the recapitulation process.

When I sat and contemplated my life, I came across many troubling memories of being criticized as a child, experiences that stripped me of my self-worth and left me with an enduring sense of shame. As I looked deeper at my past, I realized that this sense of shame was pushing me into a state of permanent defensiveness as an adult. I was always on the lookout for ways in which I was being criticized, and this made it very difficult to make friends, build a community, or engage in other activities that would help my lower cauldron heal.

I also realized that childhood trauma had frightened me out of my body, and I spent most of my adult life trapped in my head. Although I went through the normal human routines of bathing, eating, and walking around, I didn't feel a sense of innate joy or pleasure when I did these things. Instead, I numbed myself in addictive behaviors such as online shopping, desperate to escape the uncomfortable feelings in my physical vessel. These behaviors obscured my pain but did nothing to heal my trauma. I realized that my lower cauldron work had to include things like stretching, exercising, and deep breathing to help me get back in touch with my body.

EXERCISE

Shamanic Recapitulation

In your journal, write down your answers to the following questions:

Which events in your life caused you to feel unsafe, unloved, ashamed, or alone?

Which events made you feel like there was something fundamentally wrong with you?

What was missing from your childhood—friendship, nature, community, celebration?

How did these events and absences shape your view of the world?

Can you articulate any of the beliefs you may have formed as a result of these experiences that still affect your life today?

This process of recollection can be intense, so it's often better to break it up into multiple sessions. If you like, you can start with "easier" memories and work your way up to harder ones.

Pick one specific period in your childhood to start with. Let yourself remember anything about that time that comes to mind. If a difficult memory emerges, intentionally breathe out anything you took on as a result of that event—the guilt, shame, anger, or self-judgment. Next, breathe in anything that you lost as a result of that event that you wish to reclaim—for example, a sense of wonder, magic, or self-love. Feel these positive qualities flowing back to you, completely intact, just as the negative impacts are flowing harmlessly away. Allow these positive qualities to fill your lower cauldron, giving you the life force you need to grow and thrive.

By reviewing your life in this way, you can better understand why your lower cauldron is crucially depleted, which will give you important clues about what you need to do to fill it back up again. The breathing is important, but you may need some additional action, such as cutting energetic cords to a particular person or event.

Energetic Cords

If reviewing your early life experiences makes you feel angry, panicky, tearful, or overwhelmed, chances are you still have energetic cords tying you to these events, continually pulling the life force away from your lower cauldron. The concept of energetic cords can be found in shamanic traditions around the world. If you have lingering negative emotions about a person you haven't seen in decades, or if you find yourself unexpectedly yearning for a long-lost love, there is probably an energetic cord tying you to that person—a crackling thread of unresolved fear, anxiety, resentment, or lust. To be clear, not all energetic cords are bad. The cords connecting you to your friends and loved ones can be very nourishing, and completely welcome. It's the *unwanted* cords that drain your lower cauldron and leave you vulnerable to ongoing harm.

If in the previous exercise you identified an incident from your past that you just can't move beyond, or a person whose harmful words or actions are still affecting you today, you may be bound to them by a cord which is steadily draining your energy. Like a slow leak in your gas tank, or a mouse raiding your pantry while you're asleep, these cords can consume a good chunk of your life force, leaving you wondering why you can never quite seem to achieve your full potential.

I had an intense and tumultuous relationship with the father of my first child, and for years after I left him, I continued to feel an eerie connection with him. I'd see or hear things that reminded me of him, and all the old trauma would come rushing back. Sometimes, I'd have nightmares about him, or I'd run into his doppelgängers when I was out and about. No matter how hard I tried to move on, it felt like I was still available to him—like he was reaching out through the ether to scare me, or to make sure I remembered that I would never be completely free of him.

When I started my shamanic training, I had a conversation with my teacher one day in which I mentioned this relationship. She suggested that I do a cord-cutting ritual to sever any lingering attachments to my ex-boyfriend. Under her guidance, I visualized the energetic cord that was still connecting me to him. To me, this looked like a thick, heavy fire hose. Next, I visualized myself calling on a power animal to help me cut this cord. The animal who showed up from my subconscious was a little red fox with very sharp teeth. While I held the cord tight, I witnessed this fox chewing on the fire hose until it finally snapped. For a moment, the hose whipped back and forth wildly, as if electrified. Then, slowly, it began to shrivel up and fall to the ground. The part of the cord which had been attached to me likewise shriveled up, falling to pieces in my hands. I thanked the fox for helping me. Following my teacher's instructions, I visualized myself laying the remnants of the cord on the ground.

"I rededicate this energy to the earth, where it belongs," I said.

Even as I spoke those words, I knew that I would no longer be bothered by signs, coincidences, and triggers related to my ex-boyfriend. I was completely free of him now—I'd seen the cord cut with my own eyes. In the days following this ritual, I felt like I'd undergone a very successful surgery. My attachment to my ex-boyfriend had been like a tumor, steadily eating away at my life force while staying just below the radar. Now, I felt that life force returning to me, filling my lower cauldron like clear, sparkling spring water.

Cord-cutting rituals aren't just for severing unwelcome attachments to people. You can also use them to cut ties with a past event that is still causing you distress. For example, you might cut the energetic cord tying you to a car accident or other frightening experience. As you work with your lower cauldron, you may find yourself identifying a long list of events, memories, and people with whom you wish to carefully and respectfully disconnect. There is no limit to the number of reasons for which you might want to undertake a cord-cutting ritual, so take your time and work through these attachments one by one.

EXERCISE
Cord-Cutting Ritual

A cord-cutting ritual can help you move past a traumatic experience or put a toxic relationship squarely in the past. To do this, I encourage you to find a quiet space where you can sit or lie down and be undisturbed for at least thirty minutes. You will also need a drumming track (which can be found on YouTube or on my website), or your own drum if you have one.

To begin, sain your space using the practice I describe in Chapter 1. As part of your space opening ritual, you may choose to call on any Guides, ancestors, power animals, or archetypes whose assistance you would like as you embark on your cord-cutting ritual.

Next, identify the relationship or situation from which you would like to sever your attachment. Contemplate the ways this person or situation is draining your energy. Do you harbor resentment? Unrequited love? A sense of outrage or injustice?

Either play your drumming track or begin to drum slowly and steadily, and continue until your mind has relaxed and your everyday thoughts have fallen away.

Now visualize the energetic cord connecting you to the person or situation in question. Is it thick or thin? Does it look like a rope, umbilical cord, or barbed wire? What color or texture is it? Is there electricity running through it? Icky sludge? Sticky glue? How deep inside yourself does it reach? Can you pull it out on your own, or do you need help?

Next, imagine yourself cutting the cord, unravelling it, or extracting it from yourself in some way.

You may also choose to visualize your Guide, power animal, or spirit coming along to cut it for you. There may be a long process of untangling, or it may take just a few quick snips.

Feel the energy flowing back into your own body, and a sense of freedom and ease now that you are no longer energetically connected to the person or situation in question. Take your time and allow these feelings to sink in. Let yourself experience the full relief of knowing that your energy is your own.

Visualize yourself laying the cut cord on the ground and rededicating it to the earth. Resist the urge to send anything back through the cord, even well wishes or positive energy. You are here to sever the cord; that is all.

When you feel complete, give thanks to your higher self and to any spirit guides you may have called on for help. Close your sacred space, put away your drum or stop your recording, and record your impressions in your journal.

Opening to Abundance

No matter how depleted your lower cauldron may be, you can take heart in the fact that this state of depletion is *not* permanent. There is no end to the life force that is available to you, and no such thing as scarcity when it comes to refilling your lower cauldron. Just look at the way that nature is constantly replenishing itself, even under the most adverse conditions—the flowers pushing up from between cracks in the sidewalk, the birds nesting in urban chimneys, even the fuzzy green mold flourishing on a loaf of bread. You are a part of this exuberant flow of life. This is true no matter how drained, depressed, or low-energy you feel. By working with your lower cauldron, you can reestablish a felt sense of connection to this life force, and open yourself to its abundance.

Chapter 4

Lower Cauldron Work for Personal Transformation

Before I began to heal my lower cauldron, I used to dread social occasions. I had low self-esteem, and I overcompensated by being loud and boorish as I tried to show everyone that *I* was the most interesting person at the party. Meanwhile, I was terrified that anyone would find out just how small, scared, and uninteresting I really was. As a child, I'd learned that the only way to get attention from my parents was by making a scene—otherwise, I felt invisible and unlovable.

As an adult, I found myself adrift, with few close friends. My coworkers and teachers told me I was defensive, always on the lookout for ways in which I was being slighted or attacked. The truth is, I didn't feel I had the ability to handle criticism or rejection, no matter how kindly it was delivered. If anyone around me tried to communicate that my words or actions were anything less perfect, I had a meltdown.

Most of the time, it felt easier to avoid people than to run the risk of being triggered by them. I told myself I was a loner, and I cultivated a sense of superiority to the happy groups of friends I saw chatting together at restaurants or after class. To shore up my fragile ego, I told myself that I had better things to do than waste my time going to parties or attending get-togethers after work. And besides, don't shamans traditionally live at the very edge of the village, far from the madding crowd? Why should I interact with others when I could do my work perfectly well in isolation?

Then, one day, I went on a shamanic journey hoping to discover why I was still feeling so drained, even though my intuition told me that I was on the right path with my shamanic practice. The message I received was life-changing.

I sat down in my sacred space and began to drum. Slowly, my mind settled and my breath began to come more evenly. In my mind's eye, I saw myself on a small boat sailing slowly on a mist-covered lake. It wasn't long before I arrived on the shore of a beautiful island. It was dusk, and the first stars were just appearing in the sky. As I disembarked, I smelled woodsmoke in the air. Looking to my right, I saw a large group of spirits gathered around a bonfire further down the beach—horned people, wispy elves, hares with an otherworldly brightness to their eyes. I walked briskly in the other direction, avoidance being my default strategy when it came to large gatherings, but my Guide tugged on my sleeve, urging me to join the revelers at the fire.

As I walked toward the fire, a knot of anxiety formed in my chest. What would I say to the beings if they tried to talk to me? What if they saw through my defenses, and I found myself painfully exposed? Yet, when I arrived, nobody said a word. The beings to my left and right took my hands, and all at once they began to dance in a circle around the fire, pulling me with them. This dance went on for a long time. Round and round we went, our bodies merging into one great mass of celebration. My worries dissolved, and I relaxed into a sense of total oneness and belonging.

It was in that moment that I realized I had been letting my social anxiety make my decisions for me, and I was cutting myself off from the very thing I needed the most in order to repair and refill my lower cauldron: loving, connected, joyous community. Even though I hadn't grown up with solid community, and was somewhat lacking the social skills required to develop trusting relationships with others, it wasn't too late to repair this wound in my life.

After giving thanks to my Guides and closing my sacred space, I realized this was one message I wanted to put into practice right away. I decided to start attending the weekly potluck at the shamanism school where I was a student—not as the loud, boorish, fear-ridden Rhonda intent on impressing everyone, but as a regular, flawed person who might not have *anything* impressive to say. Within a few months, I'd made the first real friends I'd had in years, and I felt a newfound sense of depth and purpose in my shamanic work. Since then, I've placed community at the center of my life—and my lower cauldron is fuller than ever.

The Importance of Community

The ancient Celts lived in small villages of perhaps a few hundred people. They were bound to each other by ties of kinship and communal labor. Everyone ate more or less the same foods, sang the same songs, and knew the same myths and legends. Perhaps more than anything, their lives were defined by the landscape they inhabited. They all knew the sting of a cold winter wind and the beauty of heather blooming on the hillside.

Today, it is increasingly rare to spend one's whole life in the same place, absorbing that area's songs and stories, and giving oneself fully to the never-ending task of deep and dynamic belonging. At the same time, we have opportunities the ancient Celts never did—the ability to travel and interact with people from all over the world, the freedom to explore different subcultures and reinvent ourselves, access to a huge variety of teachers and thinkers and the communities that form around them.

Although community may look very different for us than it did for our ancestors, it is just as important today as it was back then. When we are in regular communion with other people who share our interests—whether that's spiritual development, habitat restoration, or chess—we gain access to a sense of purpose and momentum that can be hard to drum up on our own. When it comes to spiritual practices such as shamanism, regular contact with community helps to affirm and support shared values. There's a reason sangha, or community, is considered to be one of the three jewels of Buddhism—when we surround ourselves with other people who are seeking to learn and grow, our own growth is accelerated.

So what might community look like for the modern Celtic shaman? It could mean attending an online study circle where you read and discuss shamanic texts. It could mean hosting a bonfire in your back-yard and inviting your friends to take part in a ritual. It could mean meeting up with a trusted group of fellow shamans to visit sacred sites in nature. Some-times, just listening to podcasts or reading books can put you in touch with a sense of community, even if your in-person interactions with other shamans are infrequent. The key is to plug into a sense that you are not alone in this work—not in the work of sha-manism, and not in the work of life.

I have a dear friend who moved to a new town to be close to her daughter. Although she soon made some wonderful new friends, there didn't seem to be anyone there who shared her passion for shamanic practice. At first, she put her energy into yoga, book clubs, and other activities she had in common with her new friends. But after a few months, she realized there was a big hole in her life where shamanism used to be. In the absence of community, she'd stopped her regular practices of meditating and celebrating the cycles of nature. She especially missed the group rituals she used to attend with her shamanic friends. Although she knew that some shamans were per-fectly happy going solo, she realized that she needed community to support her practice.

To remedy this, she reached out to her old sha-man friends and set up a regular video conference where they could get together and discuss their practice. One of these friends told her about a shamanic weekend retreat that was coming up the following month in a town nearby. Perhaps she'd be able to make some new contacts there. The retreat proved to be exactly what she needed. She made friends with a few people who lived the next town over from her own, and they began to meet on a regular basis. Plugging back into community made her feel alive again, and her practice became more vibrant than ever.

Many of us feel ashamed if we struggle to keep up with a spiritual practice on our own—or, for that matter, with exercising, practicing a musical instrument, learning a new language, or just about any other pursuit. We worry that needing social support and external motivation means that we aren't really serious about these goals, or that we "should" be able to do it all on our own. However, throughout most of human history, it was extremely rare for a human being to attempt any of those feats alone, let alone achieve them. Humans are social animals.

The ancient Celts didn't practice shamanism in isolation, but joined together to erect standing stones, build altars, celebrate feast days, and support one another in their spiritual work. When we join together in community, we benefit from each other's struggles, insights, and moments of inspiration.

Whether you find that support online or in person, your shamanic practice will be richer and more joyful when it is connected to the sincere practice of others.

▲▼

EXERCISE
Invoking Connection

Most of us have times when we feel a deep hunger for community but, for whatever reason, are unable to fulfill it. Perhaps you just moved to a new place, or your work or family responsibilities are taking up the time and energy that could otherwise go to keeping up with friends. However, the fact that you are doing shamanic work means that you are *already* part of a worldwide community. In this exercise, I invite you to tap into this supportive web of shared vision and values.

To start, sit comfortably in a place that represents your highest aspirations as a shaman—whether that's in front of an altar in your home, in an outdoor area, or somewhere else.

Close your eyes and say out loud, "I connect to the energy of all shamans working for peace, healing, and inner transformation, wherever they may be."

Allow yourself to become aware of all the people around the world who are working toward the same goals as you—who are tending their cauldrons, working on themselves, and cultivating benevolent relationships with the natural forces that support our life on earth.

Putting a hand on your belly—the site of the lower cauldron—feel yourself connecting to the loving energy of all these shamans, and see your own energy joining this web of love.

Whether or not you ever meet your shamanic brothers and sisters, you are connected to each other through your shared work.

Allow yourself to bask in this place of connection for as long as you like.

When you feel complete, say a few words of gratitude and open your eyes.

▲▼▲

Belonging and the Lower Cauldron

Our lower cauldrons are powered by the love of our families, friends, and communities. When your lower cauldron is upright and full, you feel an innate sense of belonging. You don't worry too much about being liked, because you've come to expect that most people you meet will like you. You know who you are, where you came from, and why you're here. You have a deep sense of where home is—both in your body and on the earth.

But for many of us, that sense of home is elusive. Maybe you moved frequently as a child, never having the opportunity to put down roots; or perhaps economic circumstances forced you to leave the place you grew up, never to return. Maybe where you grew up never felt like home, and you couldn't wait to get out of there. Maybe people have always floated in and out of your life, never hanging around long enough to form the dense, protective thicket of a real community.

Even if you can't travel back in time and somehow arrange to be born in an idyllic village, surrounded by wise mentors and children who would become your lifelong friends, you can still replenish your lower cauldron by making community a central value in your life. Just like spending time in nature, creating community can feel awkward at first. But the same principles that apply to forming relationships with nature apply to people too. Namely, if you're unsure where to start, it never hurts to bring a gift—or, better yet, throw a feast.

Throwing a Feast

The ancient Celts knew the importance of feasting to establish and maintain social bonds. After all, a chieftain couldn't keep the loyalty of his warriors or allies by being stingy. A Celtic feast would feature music and poetry, cauldrons of mead, and endless trays of mouthwatering food. The Celts would feast to celebrate auspicious occasions such as the coming of spring, joining their exuberance with the abundance of nature.

A feast is a gift to the community. By throwing a feast, you give your guests a chance to meet one another and make new connections; it's a space in which to laugh, reminisce, and exchange ideas, away from the drudgery of the everyday. Feasting breaks us out of the "all work and no play" mentality which is so corrosive to the soul, and reminds us that life is for celebrating. It also breaks us out of the cycle of endless accumulation, reminding us of the joy of giving—lavishly, voluptuously, and exuberantly.

As a shamanic practice, feasting can be a way to call the nourishing power of community into your life, filling both your metaphorical and literal cauldrons. I like to throw feasts for all the traditional Celtic holy days, cooking whatever's in season and inviting my guests to bring a dish to share and an offering to toss into the bonfire or leave on the altar. Feasting with community reminds us that we're not alone—we're all on this earth together, facing similar joys and challenges through the cycle of the years.

The Celtic Fire Festivals

The Gregorian calendar did not exist for the ancient Celts. Rather than marking the exact dates of their feasts on a 365-day calendar, they determined their feast days by the length of the day, the cycle of the moon, and other markers that shifted from year to year. Below is a list of feast days they recognized and the methodology they used to determine them. These are known as the main Celtic fire festivals:

According to the Coligny calendar, a bronze plaque dating back to the second century, Samhain is celebrated on the second new moon after the autumn equinox. This is considered the Celtic new year, and is a three-day festival celebrated with bonfires. Samhain marks the end of the harvest season and the beginning of winter—a season of potential scarcity and hardship for ancient peoples, when ghosts and spirits from the unseen realms can easily cross over into this world and play tricks on human beings. Samhain often falls within two weeks of October 31. And yes, you guessed it, our modern conception of Halloween, with its skeletons and goblins and trick-or-treating, is a direct descendant of Samhain.

Imbolc is celebrated on the second new moon after the winter solstice. This festival marks the return of spring, when the goddess Brid is said to walk across the land, leaving snowdrops wherever her feet touch the ground. The word *imbolc* translates to "in the belly of the ewe," as this is a time when ewes give birth to lambs.

Beltaine takes place on the second new moon after the spring equinox. This marks the time when cattle would have been driven out to their summer pastures. The smoke from this festival's bonfires was believed to have protective qualities, and in a large-scale form of saining, people would walk their cattle through the smoke to ensure good health and growth. Householders would ritually extinguish the fires in their own hearths, relighting them with a flame from the Beltaine bonfire—a tradition that some people in Europe still practice today.

Lughnasadh takes place on the second new moon after the summer solstice. The festival marks the beginning of the harvest season, and is associated with the god Lugh. In ancient times, this festival would have included feasting and the making of offerings, and sometimes the sacrifice of a bull. There is evidence that the Celts conducted rituals on top of hills and mountains for Lughnasadh, a practice carried on by contemporary shamans today.

Even though traditionally Celtic festivals are strongly associated with marriage rites, the planting and harvesting of crops, and the fattening and slaughtering of livestock, they can still be deeply meaningful to modern, urban people. We are all cultivating and harvesting *something*, whether it's a creative endeavor, a relationship, or an aspect of ourselves that we are working on. Although we may not be literally storing up grain to last us through the winter, we still go through energetic cycles of filling our reserves, depleting them, and then filling them up again. The Celtic fire festivals are an opportunity to celebrate these natural cycles on whatever level they are taking place.

▲▼▲

EXERCISE
Throw a Feast

No matter where you live, I challenge you to throw at least one feast this year—a birthday party, a baby shower, or a celebration for Beltaine or some other Celtic festival. Try to invite at least one acquaintance you'd like to turn into a friend.

As you cook the food and prepare your space, reflect with gratitude on the occasion being celebrated and on the ways the guests have enriched your life.

Before your guests arrive, sain your space and ask for the gods to bless your feast.

At the feast, invite your guests to share songs, stories, and poetry. You might also invite everyone to take part in a small ritual, such as tossing juniper and heather into a Samhain bonfire while setting intentions for the coming year. Participating in a ritual together forges bonds that cannot be created through small talk alone, and it will give your guests a meaningful and memorable experience.

Leave a notepad by the door where guests can leave their phone numbers and email addresses, if they choose, to be shared among the attendees. This will encourage guests to stay in touch with one another after the feast and become friends.

When the feast is over, sain your space and yourself to clear any leftover energy, and rest well.

Connecting to the Earth

Feasting doesn't just strengthen social ties—it connects us deeply to the cycles of nature. In the springtime, when the flowers are blooming and the fruit is ripening on the trees, isn't it fitting that we, too, should bloom and ripen with them, filling the air with our dancing and songs? In the winter, when the plants pull their energy underground, isn't it fitting that we should gather to celebrate the mysteries of darkness—to enact the same processes in ourselves that we see in the natural world?

Modern societies are characterized by a linear progress model that eschews the reality of cycles. We see history as moving in one direction only—forward!—and tend to downplay the repetitive nature of time. In contrast, shamanic societies around the world have long recognized that life is cyclical. The energy of the earth rises and falls with the seasons; the stars wheel through the night sky; plants, animals, and people are born, grow up, and die. Honoring these cycles can be deeply comforting, because it breaks down our narrow, individualistic viewpoint, and reminds us that we are part of something greater than ourselves. While our lives are precious and worthy of celebration, they are also subject to the laws of nature—and this is a beautiful thing.

In modern times, it can be tempting to rush through milestones and special events. We might dash off a text to say happy birthday, or order takeout on holidays instead of gathering in the kitchen to cut vegetables and bake pies. When we don't take the time to celebrate and acknowledge the seasons, life can pass in a seamless blur of work and everyday tasks— a hallmark of the linear progress model. The moon waxes and wanes, and we ignore it, eyes glued to our screens. The trees leaf out, the daffodils bloom, and we realize we've missed mushroom hunting season again. The preparations that festivals require—the gathering of food, flowers, and firewood, the cleaning of the house—are a gift in their own right, putting us in deep communion with the earth. Do you know where to find fern shoots, pumpkins, juniper berries, rowan wood? Preparing for a festival draws you into the land, and shows you where to search.

A few years ago, I realized how disconnected from nature I had become. I wanted to find a certain herb to use in a ceremony but had no idea where to find it or if it was even in season. Around the same time, a friend came to visit from overseas. She peppered me with questions about the birds and animals who live on my land, and I was embarrassed to admit that I didn't know most of their names, let alone the details of what they ate and where they slept. After she left, I bought a few field guides from my local bookstore and attended a series of hikes lead by a local naturalist.

I began to spend a few minutes every morning sitting outside just watching the plants, animals, and weather, and writing down what I observed. At first, these writings felt hopelessly vague and clumsy to me: *Small brown bird on hazel tree. Raining.* But over time they took on more detail and nuance. I started to notice what the birds were doing, and what their individual calls sounded like. I realized the black, twisted rope of scat I found near the streambank was a sign that a pine marten had come by in the night. Most importantly, I became aware that thousands or even millions of other lives were taking place all around me—insect lives, bird lives, bacteria lives—and that I could learn to respect and honor those lives.

The more you get to know your local environment—its hills and trees, streams and ponds—the more you will start to become a part of that place. Just as you strengthen your ties to a human community, you will start to feel yourself part of a more-than-human community of birds, animals, and plants, and of weather systems like wind and rain. You will start to realize that, far from being a pretty backdrop, nature is an all-encompassing matrix on which you are having an effect, and which is affecting you in turn.

Grounding and the Lower Cauldron

Sometimes, shamanic journeys and rituals can bring up intense emotions. For example, I once had a student who went on a journey with the intention of finding insights to help her repair a faltering relationship—only to receive a strong, clear message from her intuition that it was time to end that relationship instead. At the end of the journey, she was crying and felt overwhelmed by this unexpected change of direction, even as she knew it was the right thing to do. She wandered around her house, feeling strange and out of sorts, unsure how to return to a "normal" state. She even began to worry that this intense journey had knocked her off-balance in a serious way. Luckily, she called an experienced friend who explained that she had become ungrounded. Her friend suggested they go for a walk in the forest together, and after walking and talking for an hour or so, she returned to a calm and centered state. Establishing a strong connection with nature can help you return to a present and grounded state even in the midst of challenging experiences—and the more time you spend in nature, the quicker your recentering is likely to be.

You probably intuitively understand what I mean by *ungrounded*—it's that floaty, flighty, sometimes panicky feeling you get when things become a little too exciting, overwhelming, or intense. For example, you might feel ungrounded after receiving a big shock, like a phone call informing you that a relative is ill. You could also feel ungrounded for positive reasons, like falling in love or receiving some long-awaited good news. From a metaphysical standpoint, becoming ungrounded occurs when you forget that your power is inside of you, and instead invest your power in whatever is happening outside of you. Grounding yourself returns your focus to the power within. Feeling ungrounded doesn't mean that anything bad is happening or that you've done anything wrong—it just means that your nervous system isn't quite keeping up with the huge amount of energy you're trying to process.

With that in mind, the best way to ground yourself is to slow down that flood of energy to a manageable level, while giving your mind and body the support they need to absorb it. For example, you might say out loud, "I am choosing to turn down the volume on this experience, and I call on the support of my higher self to do that," or "I am open to receiving this energy at a slower pace, and I ask my Guides to help make that happen." You can also add an affirmation such as, "I know that I am safe and that this intensity will pass; indeed, it is already beginning to fade away."

Next, you can support your own ability to absorb the excess energy by tapping into the grounding qualities of the earth. The earth beneath our feet is incredibly absorbent. Falling rain sinks into it; dead leaves decompose and become part of it. Likewise, the earth can absorb the energy passing through our bodies, soaking it up and helping us to feel calm and at peace. Walking barefoot on grass or dirt—a practice known in some communities as *earthing*—has been shown to reduce inflammation and promote feelings of well-being, a fact that shamanic peoples have known for thousands of years and which is now being confirmed by modern science.

One day, I was taking a walk in the hills with some friends when I spotted a piece of Scottish rose quartz poking out of the ground. It felt like the stone had called to me. While my friends waited nearby, I knelt on the ground and set to work digging it out. Although it took several minutes, and I got plenty of dirt under my fingernails in the process, I was rewarded with a beautiful, rough, pale pink stone.

At the time, I'd been struggling with an overload of intensity in my shamanic practice. I was processing a lot of childhood trauma as part of my lower cauldron work, and I'd come back from journeys feeling shaky and ungrounded. As soon as I held the stone in my hands, I felt a sense of stability and rootedness—as if the stone was transferring its own calm steadiness to me.

Since then, I've learned to keep my grounding stone in my pocket. Whenever I feel shaky, teary, or overwhelmed after a journey, I hold this stone and feel myself becoming stable, solid, and grounded. Sometimes, I imagine myself becoming a tree, with roots sinking deep into the earth. Between these two practices, it has become much easier for me to bring myself back from an ungrounded state.

If you have childhood trauma, you too may find yourself prone to becoming ungrounded during shamanic journeys or other rituals. Ungrounded states look different for everyone. Some people become very quiet and withdrawn; others become tearful or panicky; and still others become chatty and fluttery, maybe a little *too* happy or lit up. Shamanic practice is a vehicle for wisdom and growth, but it can unlock powerful energy that can feel like too much if you don't pace yourself.

If you find yourself becoming ungrounded on a regular basis, particularly during lower cauldron work, I recommend setting an intention to lower the intensity of your practice to a manageable level. You can also imagine yourself reaching out and turning down a dial, such as the volume knob on a stereo, when you find yourself getting overwhelmed. Shamanic work isn't about flooding yourself with as much energy and as many insights as possible every time you take a journey or conduct a ritual—in fact, that's a great way to burn yourself out. Slow, steady, humble work is the way to go, especially when you are still establishing a solid foundation in your lower cauldron.

Another way to protect yourself from ungrounded states is to put a little more intention into closing your space after you take a journey, do a ritual, or engage in any other shamanic practice. Take the time and space to consciously disconnect from the shamanic headspace and reconnect with the everyday world. This might take the form of a statement or invocation such as, "I now close the space and disconnect from the unseen realms," a ritual such as ringing a bell or shaking out your carpet, or all of the above. You can also imagine a portal closing or a door zipping shut, or call to mind any sound or image that helps you feel that your space is closed.

EXERCISE
Create a Grounding Ritual

It's best to have a plan in place for dealing with ungrounded states. This is because if you are already ungrounded, you may feel too flustered to come up with one on the fly. My grounding ritual consists of holding my grounding stone, imagining strong, thick tree roots connecting me to the earth, and breathing deeply. Here are some other rituals you might try:

- Spend five minutes in child's pose (kneeling with your body bent forward and your forehead against the ground), then drink a cup of hot herbal tea.

- Walk on the grass barefoot, making three slow circles around your yard or around a park, while feeling the energy of your journey or ritual slowly returning to the earth.

- Close your eyes and imagine your lower cauldron filling up with warm, nourishing broth, spreading a sense of comfort and fullness through your whole body.

- Chop some vegetables and cook an earthy, grounding soup while listening to calming music. Leave a small cup of this soup outdoors as an offering.

- Ask a friend to help you ground by doing a puzzle together, going for a walk, eating some food, or just spending some time hanging out.

- Snuggle with a cat or dog. Pets can be wonderful helpers on the path toward grounding.

You can create your own grounding ritual using any combination of these elements. The important thing is to connect with a sense of stability, safety, and gentle containment, allowing any unsettled energy to find its natural resting place once more.

▲▽

Building a Strong Foundation

By working with your lower cauldron, you lay a strong foundation for developing your two higher ones. Just as simple leg exercises are at the foundation of a ballet dancer's artistry, and simple vocal exercises are at the core of beautiful opera singing, the energy you put into your lower cauldron will support your finest and subtlest spiritual endeavours. Although it can take a lot of patient work and require you to make some significant changes in your life, the rewards of righting and filling your lower cauldron are endless.

Chapter 5

Tending the Middle Cauldron

I'll never forget the day my marriage almost ended. "Rhonda," said my husband, "your inability to say 'I'm sorry' is becoming a deal-breaker for me. I don't expect you to be perfect, but you *need* to be able to apologize sometimes—everybody does!"

I felt myself stiffening in shame and habitual defensiveness, a thick coat of armor appearing in front of my tender and vulnerable heart. *Apologize?* I thought. *If I apologize, that means admitting I made a mistake or did something bad, and if I'm a person who makes mistakes, you won't love me anymore!*

Over the next few days, I thought deeply about his comment, and about the intensity of my reaction. Waves of anxiety washed over me as I contemplated the terrifying prospect of owning up to being flawed—and the equally terrible prospect of losing my relationship with a man I loved. Then one afternoon, it hit me: *I'm not just afraid that he won't love me anymore if I'm not perfect. I'm afraid that if I'm not absolutely perfect, I won't love me anymore.*

My whole life, I'd made my self-love conditional on being perfect—or on telling myself I was perfect, anyway. I was terrified of even the mildest criticism or reprimand from others, because I thought it meant I was fundamentally bad and unworthy. I surrounded my heart with a thick stone wall because I was convinced that anyone I let over my defenses would hurt me. But my self-protective measures meant that I couldn't admit when I had hurt others—and now my husband was calling me on it.

I did some inner searching, hoping I could find some clever way around learning to apologize. Maybe I could just never do anything I had to apologize for! As you can probably guess, my inner wisdom always came back with the same message: *You're safe. It's time to face this fear.* This message came up when I sat with my drum, when I took walks in nature, and in random conversations with friends. It felt like the universe was trying to get this idea through my thick head by any means possible.

The first time I said the words "I'm sorry," I felt so anxious I thought I might throw up. You'd think I was crossing a raging river canyon on a tightrope—I was truly convinced I was in danger. I felt exposed and vulnerable, and gripped by intense fear that I was going to be shamed or attacked. Instead, my husband gave me a big hug. "Thanks for apologizing," he said. "It's okay."

I felt my heart softening. My inner wisdom had been right, of course: I *was* ready to grow past my defenses and open myself to a full range of emotions, including the sense of remorse I'd been avoiding. Since then, I've done extensive work with my middle cauldron, learning to extend love and benevolence to myself and others even when my fragile ego is being threatened. I've learned not to avoid feelings of remorse when I speak sharply or take an action I regret, but to allow these feelings to guide me to make appropriate repairs.

The ancient Celts believed that when we are born, the middle cauldron is tipped over on its side. Unlike the lower cauldron, which would ideally remain upright and full throughout your entire lifetime, it's normal for the middle cauldron's position to change in response to the ups and downs of life. Although we might aspire to keep our middle cauldrons upright and full at all times, they can get tipped over—temporarily—by things like heartbreak and grief, and our job is to learn how to patiently and lovingly set them upright as many times as necessary.

The middle cauldron can only be filled by experiencing the great joys and deep grief that life can bring. An open heart is a jewel that we must polish throughout our lifetime—not just once, but continuously. Unfortunately, instead of being taught to courageously open our hearts, many of us learn as children to keep our hearts closed and well-defended. Look at babies and toddlers—mid-tantrum, there's no doubt that a young child is feeling a wide range emotions, and they're very capable of acting them out. But at some point many of us are encouraged to tamp down these feelings, to "put on a happy face" instead of finding and cultivating true joy. We learn to "get over it" instead of completing a full cycle of legitimate grief. All too often, we are lacking in both the inner tools and the outer rituals we need to process emotions in a safe and productive way. As a result, we go around with our hearts closed, wary of letting in what we do not know how to handle. Bottling up our feelings in this way not only creates problems down the road, but it causes us to miss out on opportunities for growth.

The middle cauldron calls us to feel fully, live freely, and love fearlessly—exhortations that many of us struggle to follow, especially if we've been taught to repress our emotions, look to others for validation, and stay in our comfort zones. Working effectively with your middle cauldron means facing the truth of your inner landscape—the emotions you're avoiding, the areas in which you're holding back from meeting your true potential, the convenient lies and defenses. If, like many people, you are accustomed to holding other people responsible for your feelings, it also means taking radical responsibility for your own emotional states, and realizing that the one person who has the power to bring you lasting peace and happiness is you.

Emotions and the Middle Cauldron

The middle cauldron is where you feel and experience all emotions, from the lightest joy to the deepest sorrow. When your middle cauldron is upright and full, these emotions have a safe container in which to exist. They can burn, crackle, hum, and sparkle without hurting you or anyone else. You can witness them in their fascinating, mysterious, ever-changing glory, without having to avoid or repress a single one. Not only that, but by witnessing them from a place of love and nonjudgment, you allow even the most uncomfortable ones to transform into wisdom.

Have you ever met a person who has gone through intense grief or suffering and made it out the other side? Have you noticed how such people often possess a depth of calm and equanimity that is tangible? This is the power of the middle cauldron: the power of transformation. When your middle cauldron is balanced, you can put even the most searing grief inside of it and, with enough time and patience, that grief will be transformed into a gift.

But when your middle cauldron is tipped over, your emotions don't have a safe place to play out; there's nothing to hold them. Difficult emotions like grief can feel intractable, because the conditions are not right for them to complete the transformation process. You might find yourself getting "stuck" in emotional states with seemingly no way out. As a result, you may begin to avoid your emotions, fearful of the pain or loss of control you will experience if you let yourself feel them. Unfortunately, most of us don't live in a culture that supports middle cauldron healing. But that's why we're here. We may not be able to change the past, but we can work today on opening up our hearts again through this work.

▲▽▲

EXERCISE

Middle Cauldron Meditation

In this meditation, I invite you to find a safe container for your emotions.

To begin, close your eyes and visualize a big, strong cauldron. This cauldron might be black with soot, or made of shining silver and hammered with elaborate designs to rival the famous Gundestrup cauldron. The important thing is that your imaginary cauldron must be big enough to receive any emotion you put into it, no matter how overwhelming; and it must be strong enough to hold that emotion without cracking, shattering, or leaking.

Next, imagine yourself filling this cauldron with loving energy. This loving energy can take any form you like: glowing light, a sparkling elixir, or a dark and potent tea. Know that whatever you steep inside this energy will eventually be transmuted into love.

The next time you are experiencing a difficult or unwanted emotion, such as sadness, anger, resentment, or disappointment, visualize yourself placing this emotion into the cauldron. Let the emotion be completely submerged in the loving energy inside the cauldron.

Allow yourself to feel the emotion as completely as possible, knowing it is perfectly safe and contained within the cauldron. Let the emotion soften and change; there is no need to keep it fixed in its original form.

When you feel complete, visualize the emotion dissolving inside the cauldron, becoming one with the loving energy within.

The Four Divisions of Sorrow

The Celts realized the importance of dealing with difficult emotions, and even enumerated the ones that offered the most potential to be transformative. In *The Cauldron of Poesy*, Amergin Glúingel describes four "divisions" of sorrow that one must face in order to right one's middle cauldron and bring forth one's spiritual gifts: longing, grief, jealousy, and sacrifice. By developing your ability to fully feel and experience these four challenging states, you open yourself to receiving their treasures.

Shamanic traditions around the world recognize the value of initiation: difficult experiences that ultimately allow the shaman to reach new depths of courage, love, and personal power. For example, some Native American groups practice the Sun Dance, a physically agonizing experience that can lead to spiritual maturity. Some Zen practitioners bathe in ice water, restrict food and sleep, and go a hundred days or more without speaking a single word. Christian tradition emphasizes fasting, pilgrimages, and other forms of sacrifice.

The four divisions of sorrow can be seen as uniquely Celtic forms of initiation. Nobody *wants* to steep in the cleansing fires of longing, grief, jealousy, and sacrifice, any more than we "want" to be exhausted and dehydrated during a Sun Dance or shivering with cold on a Zen retreat—and yet when we choose these experiences and commit to them fully, they can unlock tremendous growth. Choosing discomfort teaches us that we are stronger than our fear and resistance. It shows us how to grow past our preference for pleasant, easy experiences, and learn to appreciate and even savor the difficult moments in life.

Longing

We all long for something we cannot have—a first love, the return of the old days, lost riches. Depending on its intensity, longing can be bittersweet, or it can feel like an all-consuming hunger. The ancient Celts would have been no strangers to longing; many of their songs and stories tell of women longing for their warrior husbands gone to the battlefield, men longing for the wives who have been taken from them by greedy kings, trickster spirits, or the sea, and friends who crossed over to the Otherworld, never to return.

Although longing can be a painful state, it also illuminates and clarifies your values. What you long for the most is what you care about the most—whether that's love, adventure, relationships, or a sense of connection with the natural world. Although it may be impossible to satisfy your *specific* longings (especially if your lost love is now married with three kids and living on a different continent), you can always honor the values represented by this longing. By letting yourself feel your longing completely, you allow it to transform into pure, loving energy inside your middle cauldron.

Another way to understand longing is as a form of desire. We *desire* to have our lover back, or we desire a bigger house or a "better" career. In some spiritual traditions, such as Buddhism, desire is seen as the root cause of suffering—because once we have the object of our desire, we don't remain satisfied for long, but soon begin longing for or desiring something else. Longing is rarely extinguished for good, but finds new avenues in which to persist. By observing the unquenchable nature of longing—its ever-changing forms and endless promises—we can develop the heart of wisdom.

The first step to working with longing is to closely observe how it manifests in your mind and body. Are you having obsessive, recurring thoughts about the object of your desire? What kind of story is your mind telling you? How do you feel physically? Do you feel restless, out of sorts, drained, or tearful? What would happen if you surrendered to these thoughts and feelings instead of acting on them or resisting them? Do you believe the stories your mind is telling you, or can you cultivate some space around them?

A friend of mine was in a long-distance relationship with a man who lived on the other side of the country. In between visits, she often fell prey to feelings of emptiness and impatience. It seemed like all she did in the weeks and months between visits was stare at the calendar and count down the days. Although she'd been content before getting into this relationship, her life now felt inadequate and under-stimulating. Her mind created a story that all would be well as soon as she was reunited with her love, and she felt compelled to move in with him as soon as possible so that the painful periods of separation would be a thing of the past.

Yet a quiet voice inside her whispered that this longing was a teacher whose lessons she should not dismiss. She established a habit of sitting quietly whenever those "unbearable" feelings of longing arose, giving them her full attention. Over the course of these meditations, she realized that she was putting too much of her life force into this relationship, and was neglecting her friendships and activities where she actually lived. Her life felt empty, not because it *was* empty, but because she was sending all of her energy to a person far away. Instead of making a drastic move across the country, she began to reinvest in her local friendships and community, and the longing returned to feeling romantic and bitter-sweet instead of urgent and unbearable.

Grief

The wisdom we can attain from grieving is unsur-passed in its depth. To feel and process grief is to know the depths of your human endurance. Just like longing, grieving is a universal experience that puts you in touch with all of humanity. Although grieving can be intensely lonely, it can also leave you with ties of compassion and mutual understanding to all the people you know who have likewise lost a loved one or experienced another type of deep loss. By feel-ing grief instead of repressing it, you come to terms with life's fleeting nature—also known as the law of impermanence.

The ancient Celts had extensive funeral rites at which people could express their grief in public with their friends and community. Some funerals even featured professional mourners—usually women— who would perform sorrowful songs and lamenta-tions. Their tearful keening gave voice to the sorrow of the grieving, and created a space in which people could feel comfortable weeping. While it may seem strange to us in today's world, by facilitating collec-tive grieving these professional mourners actually made it easier for communities to move on from tragedies and heal from trauma.

Like the other three sorrows, grieving expands the heart and makes us more human—if we can weather its storms gracefully, without shutting down and becoming bitter. When you have grieved, you can no longer numb yourself to another person's grief. In fact, you start to see yourself in other people, and realize that no matter how different we may look on the surface, we all suffer and feel pain. This realization is often a catalyst for living in a more kind, heartfelt, and compassionate way.

A friend of mine lost her husband to suicide after he struggled with a severe mental illness for many years. Her grief was complicated by the fact that his mental illness had deeply affected his personality, causing him to lash out in ways that made it unsafe for her to be around him during his final year. She grieved his passing, but she also grieved the deterioration of their bond before he actually died.

In the months after his death, she began to meet more and more women who had lost their partners to mental illness or drug addiction. These meetings were not intentional, but took the form of coincidences. It was as if the universe was trying to show her that she wasn't alone, that her grief was in fact shared by thousands of people around the world. She also began to meet young women who were currently in relationships with people with mental illnesses and drug addictions. She became an unofficial mentor to many of these women. Eventually, she began to lead a support group for women in this position, and her experience of deep grief became a lifeline for others.

Jealousy

Jealousy is a complex emotion that can show up as anger, suspicion, rage, fear, or humiliation. It often appears in the phrase "a fit of jealousy"—a seemingly uncontrollable state that most of us have faced at one time or another. Rooted in ego, it manifests in moments of mean-heartedness and judgment: *Why do they have what they have, and I don't? They don't deserve it. She thinks she's so hot, but she looks awful in that dress. If I had the same opportunity, I'd do it way better.* Jealousy is also deeply humbling, showing us where our insecurities lie.

An old Celtic tale tells of Queen Maeve, who is so jealous of her husband's wealth, and especially his precious white-horned bull, that she sends an army to Ulster to acquire an even more precious brown bull. Ignoring all warnings from her prophetess, the army goes to war and acquires the bull—but at great human cost. So many times, we are just like Queen Maeve: our jealousy drives us to do unreasonable things (A war over a brown bull? Really?) which we later feel ashamed of. If we can learn to hold our jealousy without reacting to it, we can transform its intensity into fierce inner strength.

On the other hand, experiencing jealousy fully can also be a deeply healing experience if you can feel the feelings and not take action from that place. If you can summon the courage to let yourself feel this difficult emotion in all its glory, it will often reward you by showing you the parts of yourself that need to be loved—your deepest fears and unhealed wounds. For example, if you feel jealous of people who had a more privileged upbringing than you, this is an opportunity to do some legitimate grieving for the ways you were (or remain) at a disadvantage, and for all those who are suffering under our deeply unequal economic system. In this sense, jealousy can act as a means of deepening your empathy and connecting you with the suffering of others.

In shamanic circles, jealousy can sometimes arise when you perceive that someone you know is having deeper or more meaningful experiences than you are. *She always gets visions on her journeys, and I don't see anything at all,* or *They always seem so calm and centered, and I'm such a hot mess in comparison.* These experiences of jealousy can be so searing, they test your trust in life. In a happy mood, you might be inclined to believe that everything happens for a reason and everyone is exactly where they are supposed to be at any given moment in time—but those beliefs can falter pretty quickly when you're confronted with the disappointment or shame that leads to jealousy.

Can you keep on believing that you're exactly where you're supposed to be on your spiritual path even when you perceive that other people are receiving gifts that you want for yourself? Can you trust in the divine wisdom of the universe when you feel deprived or unfairly passed over? Can you let yourself experience jealousy without also feeling ashamed of being jealous? These are the true tests of maturity on the spiritual path.

One of my close friends was intensely jealous when his ex-wife got together with a new partner. Although he was still floundering in the wake of their divorce, she seemed to have floated through the experience with barely a scratch and now appeared to be thriving. His mind was filled with stories about all the ways he'd encouraged and supported her throughout their relationship, only to have her new partner benefit from all his hard work and sacrifice. After doing some difficult meditation with these feelings, he realized he believed that his ex-wife owed him something for their years together, and that she had robbed him of something by leaving. This led him to an even deeper realization: that he had a lifelong habit of treating relationships as transactional and "buying" peoples' love in an attempt to feel safe.

He realized that the pain he felt had little to do with his ex-wife's happiness, and everything to do with his own feelings of unworthiness. This was a deep wound he'd been ignoring for nearly his whole life; now he had the opportunity to fully feel it and heal it. He entered therapy and began to work on this wound, learning how to love himself and others without creating a sense of debt. In his subsequent relationships, he found he was able to give and receive more freely, knowing his partners were with him because of who he was and not because of what he provided for them.

Sacrifice

Although sacrifice may be the noblest of the four sorrows, it is a sorrow nonetheless. When we make a true sacrifice, we give up something of great value with no hope of getting anything in return. Not only that, but we may feel the loss of the thing we sacrificed for many years to come. For example, if you leave a beloved home and community so that your partner can pursue a dream, or give up your career to care for a disabled child, you may mourn those losses for the rest of your life, even if you stand by the sacrifice that you made.

A traditional Celtic tale tells of a fisherman who finds a seal skin on the beach. The skin belongs to a selkie—a mythological creature that can shapeshift between seal and human form. Without it, the selkie to whom it belongs cannot return to her original seal form. She follows the fisherman home, where they fall in love and marry.

There are many different versions of this story, but in one of my favorites, the one recounted by songwriter and folklorist Gordon Bok, the fisherman goes out to sea late in the season and gets trapped in a terrible storm. His wife shifts into her seal form and swims out to save him, even though it means she can never return to her human form again. When you sacrifice for others, your heart will expand in ways you couldn't have imagined. There is something deeply humbling about knowing that your actions allowed another person to live and thrive. It wakes you up to the fact that, from the time you were born, various people in your life have made sacrifices for you, often without you even realizing it. Sacrifice puts you in touch with a great chain of giving and receiving extending back through generations, and in many cases, extending forward to future generations too.

Many years ago, one of my students received a shock when her brother, a heroin addict, asked her to adopt his two children. My friend had intentionally remained childless and had never expected to take on the responsibility or financial burden of raising a family. Yet it was clear that her brother and his girl-friend could not give the children a safe and healthy home, tangled up as they were in their addictions. After processing her fear, resistance, and resentment, she realized that she was willing to sacrifice the child-free future she had envisioned in order to give her niece and nephew a better life.

Taking care of the children was not easy. She had to find a new living situation and give up much of her free time to help the kids with homework, pack their lunches, and take them to playdates on week-ends. Not only that, but the kids seemed oblivious to how much their aunt had sacrificed, and were any-thing but grateful for the care she lavished on them. She had to learn the hard way how to give without expecting anything in return—the definition of sac-rifice. More than a decade later, when the kids had become adults and left home, she received a call from the older one.

"I just want to say thank you," he said. "I never realized how much you had to give up to take care of us when we were kids. But when I imagine someone asking me to do what you did, it's almost unthinkable. You gave us a chance at life, and I will always be grateful."

Whether or not you ever receive a direct expression of gratitude from the person or persons for whom you sacrificed, know that your energy did not go to waste. Your energy is out there, contained by the web of life in ways you can't even imagine, rippling out to support the lives of countless beings. Sacrifice teaches us to surrender to the mysteries of existence—mysteries that transcend mere accounting. The ability to submit to mystery is a hallmark of shamanic mastery.

EXERCISE
Working with the Four Divisions of Sorrow

One beautiful way to work with the four sorrows is through ritual. Rituals allow us to express through gestures and symbolism what can't always be conveyed with words alone.

To begin, take some time to identify the ways these four sorrows are playing out in your life right now. You can do this by asking yourself these questions and answering them in your journal:

What am I longing for?

What am I grieving?

What makes me jealous?

What have I sacrificed?

Over the next few days, collect a small object to represent each one of these sorrows—for example, a stone from a riverbed, a piece of jewelry, or anything else that holds significance to you.

Once you have gathered all four objects, find a quiet place to sit with them. Taking each object in your hand one by one, make a spoken invocation affirming your intention to allow these experiences to expand your heart. For example,

May the longing I feel deepen my empathy for all those who yearn for what they cannot have.

May my grief serve as a reminder that life is fleeting.

May my jealousy give me compassion for those who are jealous of me.

May my sacrifice teach me to put my love into practice.

As you speak these words, allow yourself to feel the strength and warmth of your sturdy middle cauldron holding these intentions for you.

If you are working with any Guides, take a moment to visualize them and ask for their help in fulfilling your intentions.

You can complete the ritual by burning incense, shaking a rattle, or doing anything else that feels significant to you.

If you feel yourself getting overwhelmed, you can sit with your power objects, recall your intentions, and commit these sorrows to your middle cauldron. You can also create a similar ritual to deal with any difficult emotions. By stating a positive intention for a challenging emotional state, you transform its poison into personal power.

Seeing Life Through Shamanic Eyes

Working with the four sorrows teaches us to value all aspects of life, including the difficult ones. We realize that every experience in life can be a teacher if we allow it to be. Before I discovered shamanism, it was very easy for me to get knocked off-balance by the unexpected bumps and bruises of life. If things didn't go according to my plan, I would panic, convinced that my life was headed for disaster. By working with the four sorrows, I began to realize just how often the so-called setbacks in my life were blessings in disguise.

For example, the grief I experienced after my father's death galvanized my commitment to becoming a strong presence for my younger siblings. The jealousy I felt after a friend bought a beautiful house in the countryside helped me empathize with and ultimately forgive another friend who was jealous when my social media channel started taking off. By dedicating these experiences to my middle cauldron, they really did expand my heart and deepen my compassion for other human beings.

I still experience difficult emotions when things don't go my way, but they tend to be fleeting, and are swiftly replaced with curiosity. I'm getting better at saying, "That's interesting. I wonder what happens next?" instead of declaring my life ruined.

Learning to see with shamanic eyes means looking out for the little winks and nudges the universe is constantly giving us, while holding our own opinions with gentle skepticism or even humor—in other words, remembering that they're *just opinions*. I have a friend who used to hitchhike everywhere when she was younger and had wonderful stories about her adventures. Once, I called her on the phone, and she told me that her car had broken down in a town an hour away from where she lived. "That must have been awful," I said, my mind flooding with anxiety on her behalf. "Oh no," she replied. "I had a great time getting home. I forgot how much I loved hitching rides with strangers—it made me feel young again."

When we set aside our negative opinions about the events in our lives—not discard them, exactly, but recognize that they are only one possible response among many—we open ourselves to unexpected sources of wisdom and joy. Opinions are limiting: they cause us to look at the world through a narrow lens. All too often, that narrow lens is based on our fears, mental habits, and societal conventions. We anticipate pain and discomfort and preemptively guard ourselves against those things, instead of approaching life with a sense of curiosity. As the Buddhist teacher Sengcan wrote, "The great way is not difficult for those who have no preferences." This is just as true for shamans as it is for Buddhists!

EXERCISE
Gratitude Practice

Consciously expressing your gratitude on a regular basis is a wonderful way to keep in touch with joy. Western science now supports what mystics have been saying for thousands of years: an attitude of gratitude is key to a happy and fulfilling life. In this exercise, I invite you to practice gratitude in a couple of different ways.

Journaling

First, in your journal, make a list of things that bring you joy. Use all five of your senses when making this list, being sure to include sounds, sights, smells, tastes, and touches that delight you, as well as interactions with other people.

Next, read the list out loud. There is something special about speaking and hearing your own gratitude list; it makes it more real and memorable, and helps call a sense of gratitude into your body, not just your mind.

When you're finished reading your list, sit quietly in meditation for a few minutes, allowing the warm feeling of gratitude to sink in.

Do this practice every morning for the next two weeks, and see if you don't notice feeling more grateful throughout the day.

Working with the Four Sorrows

The next time you work with one of the four sorrows, see if you can find gratitude for that specific sorrow in addition to any other feelings you may have about it. We are complex creatures who have the ability to hold multiple feelings at the same time, and about the same situation.

For example, the next time you feel jealous of someone, can you simultaneously feel happy for them too? When you long for something or someone, can you also be grateful for the strength of will you are gaining by living without the object of your desire? When you grieve over the death of a loved one, can you feel gratitude that they are at peace in the

Otherworld? When you sacrifice something, can you feel gratitude for whomever your sacrifice benefits?

Practice feeling gratitude for the compassion that all of these experiences create in you. There are myriad ways to practice gratitude for the four sorrows. I invite you to further explore the treasures of this work.

▲▼▲

Joy and the Middle Cauldron

The middle cauldron isn't only home to the four sorrows—it is also the place where we feel and cultivate joy. In our busy modern world, joy can feel like an old-fashioned sentiment, something we hear about in Christmas carols but rarely experience in "real" life. Indeed, sometimes it feels like Western culture values suffering far more than joy. We revere our tortured poets and suicidal rock musicians, our violent movies and tragic novels. In some cases, we may even start to feel like if we're not suffering enough—in our work, our relationships, or otherwise—that there must be something wrong.

Yet if you look at the lives of the Celts and other shamanic peoples, joy was valued very highly indeed. Songs of praise proliferated. In fact, one of the earliest recorded pieces of Celtic poetry, the *Song of Amergin*, hums with the joy of being alive in a living world. It consists of a series of "I am" statements, followed by a vivid description of an animal or natural feature found in Celtic lands—a wild boar, a salmon, a particular kind of wind or rain.

Amergin's poem is a celebration—not only of being alive, but of existing in communion with so many beautiful living things. The bard invokes one powerful natural force after another, summoning those qualities to himself, in an incantation that, spoken aloud, would sound a lot like casting a spell. There is something ecstatic to this relentless naming of plants, animals, and wild features—you can tell the poet has real relationships with all of these things, relationships which bring him meaning, strength, and joy. On the deepest level, the poet is expressing his oneness with all of these things. The idea that all things are one is present in the mystical aspect of almost every major spiritual tradition, and it's no surprise to see this idea expressed so beautifully by an ancient Celtic bard.

Yet to modern, socialized ears, this poem might sound simplistic. *Okay*, we might say, *but where's the conflict? Where's the trauma?* We're so used to seeking out what is difficult and complicated that we miss the pleasure of letting things be easy. Instead of letting joy blossom, filling our middle cauldrons with its warm and radiant light, we hunt for the negative, and let our fears and anxieties run the show. To right and fill our middle cauldrons, we must learn how to invite joy back in.

▲▼

EXERCISE
Cultivating Joy

In this exercise, I invite you to deeply appreciate your favorite aspects of the natural world.

Go for a walk in your favorite park or natural area. Every time you see something beautiful—be it a flower, insect, bird, or animal, or the sparkle of light on water—stop, give that thing your full attention, and say a few words of appreciation.

For example, "Look at your beautiful feathers! Look at how they shine in the light. And the way your throat moves when you sing. I love you."

At the same time, imagine that the thing you are beholding is likewise beholding you and appreciating *your* beauty. What do you think it would say?

Allow yourself to feel deep communion with the plant, animal, or natural phenomenon with whom you are engaging. Feel joy flowing from your heart when you reflect the beauty of nature back upon itself, and flood it with appreciation.

▲▼

Opening to Emotions

The middle cauldron invites us to open ourselves to the full range of emotions, and to fully savor the universal experiences that help us to mature as human beings. By leaning into these experiences instead of shrinking back from them, you develop the gift of courage—a gift which helps you to be strong for others, not only for yourself. Opening yourself to the joys and sorrows of life is also the mark of a true artist: after all, you can't convincingly express what you've never allowed yourself to feel. Celtic bards knew well the importance of an upright middle cauldron for creating masterpieces, and this is as true today as it ever was.

Chapter 6

Middle Cauldron Work for Personal Transformation

Before I discovered my calling as a shaman, I was an accountant rising through the ranks of the corporate world. After going through a period of financial precarity in my early twenties, I was making great money and had a home, pension, and many other trappings of success. If my heart was telling me there was something more to life, I tuned it out. Then one day, a friend invited me to attend a workshop on shamanism. It was summertime, and the workshop took place outdoors on a beautiful piece of land filled with rowan and birch trees. Sitting in a circle with the other participants, listening to the teacher beat a simple rhythm on a frame drum, I felt something inside myself unlocking which had been locked up for a very long time.

After that workshop, I began to spend more and more time in nature. Sometimes I would go for walks, and sometimes I'd just sit still. The more time I spent in nature, the more I began to value my relationships with birds, bugs, streams, and stones — relationships that were hard to cultivate from inside my cubicle at work. I also began to place more of my focus on inner transformation, using the shamanic principles I'd learned in the workshop. As I slowly began to feel more self-love and take more responsibility for my own well-being, I realized how much I wanted to center my life around the values of kindness, service, and sacrifice — not exactly priorities in the corporate world.

As my values came into sharper focus, I was faced with a choice: ignore them, and continue on my current trajectory, or embrace them, with all the risk and uncertainty that entailed. Friends and acquaintances had been telling me that I had a gift — but was a gift a good enough reason to turn my whole life upside down? Little by little, I began to put more of my energy into shamanic practice, until one day I realized I was ready to take the leap in a bigger way. I put in my notice at my job and devoted myself to my undeniable vocation — teaching and practicing Celtic shamanism full-time.

Although the words *coire erma* are frequently translated as "the cauldron of motion," an equally popular alternate translation is "the cauldron of vocation." The middle cauldron is where you hold your soul's purpose in this life. When your middle cauldron is upright, you can live your soul's purpose and let it shine out for others to see—but when your middle cauldron is tipped over for long periods of time, your soul's purpose may be hidden underneath it, where it feels safe and protected but never gets a chance to be expressed.

Spiritual traditions around the world have long acknowledged the fact that the brain is not the only "mind" in the body, and modern science has revealed that the stomach and the heart are also the sites of various kinds of thinking and awareness. Think of the last time your brain told you that all was well, but your gut instinct warned you to be wary—or when your brain tried to convince you of a decision based on logic, only to be trumped by a pang in the heart. The Celts, too, were attuned to this triumvirate of awareness, and this is reflected in their emphasis in developing all three of your cauldrons.

When I was contemplating my decision to leave my corporate job, I decided to take a cue from the ancient Celts and check in with all three of my cauldrons—but most of all with my middle cauldron and the wisdom of my heart. If I listened to my "heart brain," where would it steer me? As you are reading this book, the answer was clear—my middle cauldron instructed me to devote my life to practicing and teaching Celtic shamanism. My lower cauldron agreed, letting me know that it contained the necessary reserves to power this venture. Finally, I consulted my upper cauldron. Could my "head brain" support this endeavor? After throwing up a few fear-based objections, the answer that came back was yes, it could. In fact, my "head" brain became a tremendous ally in the transition from accountant to shaman, helping me with the nuts and bolts of changing my life and taking a leap into the unknown.

Finding Your Vocation Using Celtic Archetypes

Some of us were born knowing our vocations. As soon as we were old enough to hold a pencil, swing a hammer, or assist in removing a splinter, we kept going and never turned back. For others, vocation can feel more elusive. It can be hard to separate your true vocation from the voices of your parents, teachers, and relatives, who may have encouraged you to do or be a specific thing. How do we get past the layers of socialization, the well-meaning nudges toward one path and warnings against other ones, the voices in our heads telling us not to "waste" our education or "risk" taking the road less traveled, and discover the calling of our hearts?

Sometimes, finding your vocation feels like getting struck by lightning. You wander into the "wrong" classroom, bump into a friend who's heading to an event and invites you to come, or help a neighbor finish a project, not realizing that your life's purpose is about to come into sharp focus. Other times, a vocation can be like an ancient sword buried in stone, requiring patience and care to excavate. Of course, our vocation may change over time, like the seasons of our lives, but regardless of whether your vocation emerges slowly or in one bright flash, chances are it falls under one of four archetypal pathways: that of the warrior, the bard, the healer, or the scholar.

> **Warriors** are those who feel called to protect the weak and vulnerable, and to fight for justice. If you have a vocation as a warrior, you might find your calling in social work, activism, or public service. Warriors go where others fear to tread, confronting the forces of delusion, greed, and inequality. You may frequently find yourself standing up for others and for the environment. You might also possess the strength of a fierce warrior in your

shamanic work, transforming fear through the power of unconditional love.

Bards are those who feel called to serve their communities through poetry, song, writing, and other forms of art. Although this might sound like an easier path than that of the warrior, this couldn't be further from the truth. Bards are often tasked with holding their community's stories, including difficult and traumatic ones, and transforming them into medicine which can heal ruptures and bring about forgiveness. If you are called to the path of the bard, you might find yourself using your creative gifts in your shamanic work, such as by making spontaneous invocations or connecting with the sacred through music or song.

Healers are those who are deeply attuned to the suffering of others, and adept at locating the seen and unseen causes of this suffering. Often, they have gained this skill as a result of deeply examining and gently releasing their own inner wounds. If you are a healer, you may find yourself drawn to becoming a doctor, counselor, or therapist. You might also find yourself sharing your healing gifts through less formal means, by acting as a shoulder to cry on for your friends, or providing caring mentorship for a child. In shamanic practice, you may find yourself drawn to cord-cutting and other healing rituals which let you release deeply held fears and unlock the love within.

Scholars are those who feel drawn to seeking knowledge beyond that which is found in ordinary books or classes, and using that knowledge to serve their community. A scholar's inquiries will often take him or her on long journeys, be they across distant lands, through the pages of obscure texts, or down deep rabbit holes of old recordings. Scholars retrieve what has been forgotten, bring truths to light, and recover the wisdom of past ages. If you have a scholar's vocation, you may find yourself developing an exhaustive knowledge of Celtic folklore, herbal medicine, or another complex field, and delivering that knowledge to your community in a form they can benefit from and understand.

As you read over these four descriptions, did any one in particular resonate for you? What do you feel in your middle cauldron as you consider each path? For many people, it can be a combination of all four, with some leading the way or feeling more dominant in certain situations or times in your life. For example, a friend of mine who'd spent twenty years as a firefighter saw herself as a warrior. But when she worked with this exercise, she remembered the time her brother was struggling with severe depression and she'd moved in with him for a few months—embodying the heart of a healer. She also remembered the intensity with which she'd studied physics when she was in high school, and the beautiful, poetic speech she'd written for her sister's wedding. She realized she wasn't limited to one archetype, but accessed the gifts of each one at different moments in her life.

Here, again, it's important to think about life as a cycle rather than a linear progression. You may feel more like a warrior at work and a bard in your creative practice at home. With friends from your shamanic circle you may adopt the scholar role, and in your family of origin you may be called to be the healer—especially if you grew up in a dysfunctional environment. There are many ways to feel and express the archetypes in your life, and by thinking about them and identifying them within yourself you will likely find you become better at each of these vocations. It will also help bring balance to your middle cauldron.

EXERCISE

Journaling on the Archetypes

In your journal, I invite you to answer the following questions:

When in your life have you been the warrior?

When have you been the bard?

When have you been the healer?

When have you been the scholar?

Take your time with this and write out any specific details that come to mind. Although you may identify strongly with one particular archetype, this exercise can surprise you by showing the ways you embody all four.

After you write down your answers to each prompt, take a moment to feel into each one of them, placing your emphasis on your heart and gut instead of your head. Which archetype brought you the most joy? Which archetype brought something less than joy? Once you know what makes your heart sing, you can lean more into that.

▲▼

Removing the Obstacles of the Heart

Realizing your vocation and living it don't always happen at the same time. In fact, many of us have to conquer significant internal and external obstacles before we are able to realize our vocations—and the most common form these obstacles take is fear. Fear is the voice that tells you that you're not good enough to fulfill your calling, and that it's not even worth trying in the first place. It's the voice that says you're too weak to be a warrior, too wounded to be a healer, too dense to be a scholar, and too ordinary to be a bard.

Often, our fears have good intentions. They want to protect us from pain, shame, and failure—never mind the fact that, in doing so, they are simultaneously "protecting" us from realizing our deepest gifts. Fear can feel so urgent that many of us are in the habit of simply following its directives, no matter how deeply they may contradict our values or point us away from our goals. We feel a sense of discomfort in our bodies, or have a thought beginning with the words "What if . . ." and before we know it, we're closing our hearts and retreating to familiar ground—no matter how cramped and unpleasant it may be. It's easy to forget that what's familiar is not always what's true. And fear can muddle this for us, with ill effects.

One of the most important skills we can learn on the shamanic path is to relate to our fears in a new way—not as commanders to be obeyed or enemies to be conquered, but as messengers letting us know where we need to heal and grow. Viewed in this light, our fears are very valuable! But all too often, we react to them blindly instead of slowing down enough to listen to what they have to teach.

Have you ever tossed out a piece of mail by accident, not realizing it contained an important document or even a check? In some ways, this describes our life-long relationship with fear. We deal with it in a hurry, doing whatever we can to return to a state of real or imagined safety, never realizing that all along we've been throwing away something important, a tool that has the power to change our lives. When we can sit with our fear without reacting to it, fear transforms into a teacher—and its lesson is unconditional love.

Sometimes, our fears can be lurking so far beneath the surface that we never consciously articulate them—we just live them out, week after week and year after year. For example, you might keep romantic partners at a distance, telling yourself, "He's not really serious about me," or "If she really loved me, she'd do [blank]," never realizing that these doubts stem from a deep fear that nobody could possibly love you. You might spend an entire lifetime coming up with what sound like perfectly reasonable critiques of other peoples' behavior, while all along it is your fear of being unloved that is running the show.

Once you identify these subterranean fears, it can be astonishing to realize the extent to which they've been narrowing your field of vision and determining what is possible for your life. You might discover that decisions that felt like "yours" were actually made by your fears—as if a little team of gremlins commandeered your life years ago and never gave it back. But with practice you can come to know the difference between actions and decisions you are taking out of fear, and those which are coming from your higher self.

One good way to do this is to check in with your body. Does your heart feel open, tender, and loving as you take this action or make this decision? Or does it feel closed, anxious, or defensive? In other words, are you connected to a sense of vulnerability—the possibility that you could get hurt—or are you concerned with avoiding pain at all costs? If you realize you are coming from a place of fear, there's no need to beat yourself up. Simply pause, feel deeply into your middle cauldron, and ask yourself if you can return to this question or decision at a later time, once you've had the chance to tap into a sense of love and support. By checking in like this on a regular basis, you can come to know the "flavor" of your higher self—and once you know it, you will never again confuse it with the flavor of fear.

△▽

EXERCISE

Tapping into Your Higher Self

If you've realized that you're speaking or acting from a place of fear, you can reconnect with your higher self by using this simple exercise.

To begin, close your eyes and place one hand on your belly and one hand on your heart. This posture draws on the nourishing power of the lower cauldron to support the middle cauldron.

Stay here for a minute or two, feeling the way your lower cauldron is strong and steady, holding up your middle cauldron from below.

Allow yourself to feel safe, as if you were being wrapped in a warm blanket, held by strong arms, enfolded by fairy wings, or any other image that evokes that feeling for you.

When you are ready, say the words, "I call on the wisdom of my heart to make this decision/answer this question/take this action. I trust in my higher self to do the right thing."

At this point, you may feel a wave of emotion such as sadness or worry. These are the feelings your fear was trying to protect you from. Keeping your hands on your heart and belly, allow these feelings to bubble up and make themselves known. Trust that your lower and middle cauldrons, working in harmony, are completely capable of handling these feelings in a safe, non-traumatizing way.

When you feel complete, allow yourself to feel your consciousness located in your heart space. Know that this heart mind is always there to guide you.

▲▼▲

Boundaries

The more you work with your fears, the more you will start to notice the ways they define your interactions (or lack of interactions) with other people. For example, you may be in the habit of giving too much because you're afraid that people won't love you outside of your ability to provide for them; or you may keep walls up out of fear that others will reject you if they see how weak and vulnerable you are inside. As you cultivate your middle cauldron, and grow more confident in your ability to discern the voice of fear from the voice of your higher self, you may find yourself wanting to reassess your boundaries, or to establish new boundaries where there were none before.

When I first began to offer shamanism courses at my home in Scotland, I had one particular student who was always in crisis. He would call me up in tears to tell me about a difficult journey he'd taken, or to confide his fears about a ritual gone wrong or his anxieties that he was "too broken" to open himself to divine guidance. At first, I gave him a great deal of time and attention, listening to his worries (often at length) and giving him my best advice for how to proceed. As time went on, however, I began to feel drained. As a single crisis morphed into a never-ending state of neediness, I realized I needed to set better boundaries.

My fear told me that if I set a boundary, I would be abandoning this student—leaving him in peril when I ought to be jumping in to save the day. But when I tapped into my heart mind, I perceived that he was no longer reaching out to me from a place of genuine need, but as a bid for attention I didn't have the time or energy to give. The next time he called me "in crisis," I asked him to reflect on whether he was truly working with the shamanic practices I was teaching him, or if the shamanism course had become an arena in which he could play out old scripts about needing to be seen. I asked that he stick to the basics and refrain from taking the kind of intense journeys that kept landing him in crisis again and again. Finally, I let him know that I was available for genuine questions about shamanic practice via email, but that I could not be on call as his around-the-clock coach and counselor.

Although this may sound harsh, I was quite aware, as I spoke, that my middle cauldron was standing upright. It takes vulnerability to admit to a person that they are bothering you, and to risk having them accuse you of being cold and uncaring. But this combination of vulnerability and firmness is far better than a false generosity predicated on fear. As it happened, my student heard that he was asking for too much and agreed to confine his shamanic practice to a level he could handle safely on his own. At the end of our conversation, I felt a sense of love and respect for both myself and my student—far better than the strain and resentment that were creeping in before.

▲▽

EXERCISE
Power Animals for Boundary Setting

We can look to the animal world for good examples of boundary setting. Wolves, bears, and other creatures feel no guilt or shame about protecting their territory or resources. These animals will not hesitate to let intruders know when they have crossed a line, and they set boundaries clearly by scratching marks onto trees, urinating in specific places, or vocalizing to say, "Anyone who hears this song or howl, know that this is my turf!"

Humans are the only animals who wring our hands over boundaries, second-guessing ourselves and taking too much responsibility for other peoples' reactions. In this exercise, I invite you to tap into the confidence of a power animal to assist you in setting boundaries.

To begin, think of an animal who represents strength, confidence, and shamelessness to you. Alternatively, you can play your drum and meditate until a power animal comes forward for you.

Meditate on the qualities of this animal. Is it big? Fierce? Strong? Confident?

Allow yourself to feel those qualities in your body.

The next time you need to set a boundary, take a moment to invoke this power animal. You might hear it growling, see its eyes sparkling, or imagine its posture when defending its territory.

Allow yourself to feel that this power animal has your back as you set a healthy boundary.

Forgiveness and the Middle Cauldron

Setting strong, appropriate boundaries sets you up to do another important middle cauldron task: forgiving those who have hurt you. Having good boundaries makes it safer to forgive others, because you are clear that forgiving someone does not necessarily mean letting that person back into your life, and it certainly doesn't mean allowing that person to abuse or take advantage of you.

When someone has hurt you, memories of the hurtful event can take up a lot of mental and emotional energy. Like a box of old clothing you store in your basement, old hurts take up a lot of valuable space, and the return on investment may be lower than you assume. Shamans know that everything is energy. This energy can either be trapped and unavailable, or it can be flowing and available. Old hurts represent trapped energy that cannot be put to higher use. Until you learn the power of forgiveness, some part of your energy will always be tied up in maintaining those wounds.

Anger, whether repressed or expressed, is an issue many of my students struggle with. I often find that their anger is a surface emotion that, when faced, gives way to feelings like disappointment, loneliness, or resentment. One student was harboring a lot of hurt and anger about the way his parents had prioritized work over family when he was a child. While other kids' parents helped him with homework and played with him on the weekends, his parents were obsessively focused on growing their business, putting all their energy into this endeavor even beyond the point of real financial need. Now that he was an adult and had children of his own, his parents had retired from their business and were eager to be highly involved grandparents. However, he found it hard to let them shower the kind of love and attention on his children that they had never given to him. Not only that, but he resented how much his children loved his parents, and even found himself wanting to sabotage that relationship.

Luckily, he had enough self-awareness to know that acting on his resentment could only result in deeper damage for everyone involved. Not only that, but he knew that it would be a terrible waste to deprive his children of a relationship with loving grandparents, no matter what his own childhood experience had been. Still, the resentment continued to dog him, souring what would otherwise be beautiful moments with his family.

Then one night after meditating for a long time, he fell asleep and had a dream in which he saw himself standing with his parents under an enormous oak tree with a thick, leafy crown. Sunlight was filtering down through the leaves, and translucent specks of pollen were drifting through the air. He had the strong, unspoken sense that his life and his parents' lives were contained within a force of love that was bigger than any one of them. In the context of this huge and all-containing love, his resentment felt meaningless. In the dream, he could scarcely remember why he'd been angry at all.

When he woke up, he decided to invite his parents to go on a walk with him. As they strolled beneath the oak and maple trees, he said, "Mom, Dad, I want you to know that it's been really hard for me to watch you showering my kids with so much attention. I feel jealous of them for getting what I did not. I want to move past my anger, but I need your help."

Before he could say any more, his parents began talking about how much they regretted spending so much time on their business when he was a child, and how they hoped to make it up to him by being great grandparents. What he experienced as unfairness was actually their desperate attempt to make amends for their previous mistakes. As he listened to them talking, he felt a deep sense of relief washing through him. He realized he could forgive them after all. By the end of their walk, he felt as though his former resentment had been soaked up by the trees, the same way they soak up carbon dioxide from the atmosphere. His heart felt open, and his energy had been returned to him, clean, fresh, and available to use in a joyful, productive way.

EXERCISE

Forgiveness Writing and Visualization

If there is someone you want to forgive, try this writing exercise combined with an intentional visualization.

To begin, find a quiet spot where you will be undisturbed for the next thirty minutes and where you can sit or lie down comfortably. Take a few deep breaths and let yourself become fully present. Next, call to mind the person against whom you are harboring anger or resentment, as well as the situation that is still on your mind.

Then imagine that you are meeting this person's higher self with your higher self in the ethereal realm. In other words, imagine this person's highest version of themselves, without the baggage of their addictions, anger, or mental conditions that allowed them to behave in the way they did toward you. Under ideal conditions, what would this person say to you? Would they apologize? Could you feel and accept this apology? What would you say to this person in return? Write this imaginary dialogue down in your journal.

After imagining this conversation between your highest selves, close your eyes and allow yourself to feel seen, heard, and validated by this person in the form you most desire. When you feel complete, open your eyes and reconnect with your surroundings. There is no need to take any further action or contact the person in question; forgiveness is for *you*, and by working with this exercise, you can reclaim the energy that was previously going into holding on to hurt.

▲▼▲

Tending the Cauldron of Motion

When we tend our middle cauldron with courage and compassion, we make ourselves available to life instead of fortifying ourselves against it. There is no need to fear life—its joys and sorrows, disappointments and unexpected turns—when you are equipped with a strong middle cauldron. When it is properly nourished by the lower cauldron, and in harmonious balance with the upper cauldron, you can be confident that your "heart mind" can guide you through any situation, becoming one of your greatest treasures as a shaman.

Chapter 7

Activating the Upper Cauldron

My mind used to be a very uncomfortable place. Like a run-down urban bus station, it was always filled with familiar characters I desperately wanted to avoid: stressed-out commuters, self-aggrandizing drunks, gossips with their cell phones pressed to their ears, paranoiacs. How to tame this cacophony of fears, worries, repetitive thoughts, and self-serving schemes? My solution was to surround myself with other people (whose own minds were surely saner and more serene than mine) and never allow myself to be alone with my thoughts. When other people weren't available to distract me, I distracted myself with online shopping, binge-watching TV, and anything else that would drown out my internal noise.

It took me a long time to realize that by avoiding my own mind and refusing to face the discomfort of my inner landscape, I was allowing a big part of my intelligence to go to waste—not to mention my creativity. By perceiving my own thoughts as being real and threatening, I gave them too much power, not realizing that my real power lay in the all-encompassing awareness beyond those thoughts. Slowly and painstakingly, I began to befriend my mind, learning to listen beyond the noise to the stillness and benevolence within. Over time, my upper cauldron became a nicer and nicer place for my consciousness to reside—and I gained access to the creative intelligence which had been drowned out before.

The upper cauldron, known as the cauldron of wisdom, is located at the level of the head—home of your brain, your pineal gland, and other portals to the divine. Celtic shamans associate this cauldron with *imbas forosnai*—the divine inspiration that gives poets their songs and artists their visions. This cauldron is also associated with thinking, planning, worrying, and other mental activities. When it is well-supported by the lower and middle cauldrons, the upper cauldron can assist us in developing our full spiritual and intellectual potential; without solid support from the other cauldrons, we can end up anxious, trapped in mental loops, or overwhelmed by an influx of spiritual experiences.

The ancient Celts believed that in the afterlife the gods took your upper cauldron and tipped it upside down, emptying out all of your memories from previous lives (yes, the Celts believed in reincarnation). The purpose of emptying the upper cauldron is to give your soul the chance to start over. This is why Celtic shamanism does not emphasize past-life regression or related practices—our upper cauldrons were tipped over to *prevent* us from remembering past lives, so there's little point in trying to chase them down. Although some Celtic shamans believe that people born into shamanic or bardic lineages have an easier time turning their upper cauldrons upright than everyday folks, the fact remains that we are all born with this cauldron turned upside down.

Unlike the lower cauldron, which supports our lives most effectively when it is upright and full, the upper cauldron isn't meant to be upright and full at all times. Think of a peak experience you've had, such as rafting a fast-moving river or experiencing a state of sexual or spiritual ecstasy. As intense and precious as those experiences may be, you wouldn't want them to last twenty-four hours a day, every day (although some adrenaline junkies do exactly that, with perilous results). When it comes to upper cauldron opening, there is such a thing as too much. The point here is to be balanced. You want to be able to turn over your upper cauldron and access those exalted states when needed, while keeping it turned safely downward at other times.

Many shamanic students are in a hurry to work with their upper cauldrons. We want to have those peak experiences and download those spiritual insights which can feel so elusive when we're deep in the trenches of our everyday lives. We want to bypass the seemingly mundane work of tending to our relationships, looking honestly at our fears, and shedding our self-limiting habits, and jump straight to a heightened state in which the world seems charged with mystical inspiration.

But the upper cauldron's treasures only become available when the lower and middle cauldrons are well-nourished and working in harmony. For example, if your lower cauldron is drained and you feel chronically ungrounded, it will be much harder to cultivate a state of clarity and brightness in your upper cauldron. If you are harboring resentments or feelings of low self-worth in your middle cauldron, the insights of the upper cauldron won't do you much good. For this reason, I teach all my students to spend as much time as possible working with the lower and middle cauldrons, allowing the upper cauldron to open in its own time, at its own pace.

Working with the Mind

Before attempting to right the upper cauldron, spend some time with it in its tipped-over state. In other words, pay attention to the everyday activity of your mind. What's going on in there? Do you spend a lot of time planning? Worrying? Playing out regrets for the past or fears for the future? Does your mind feel calm and expansive, or cramped and noisy? How does it change from moment to moment and from day to day? Do you believe your own thoughts, or can you hold them with a healthy skepticism, no matter how convincing they may sound? Can you tell the difference between thoughts that come from a place of fear and thoughts that originate in your higher self?

Although the mind can feel like a single, cohesive voice or personality, it's usually more of a cacophony. Sometimes, your fearful self has the microphone; then your expansive self will get a turn for a few minutes. Your jealous self may pipe up with an opinion, only to be placated by your wise self. Each self can feel equally real and urgent—resulting in a contradictory mess of instincts. The first step in working with your upper cauldron is to simply pay attention to which self is talking. Do you want to listen to your jealous self or your fearful self, or wait patiently until your wise self comes online?

Just as the two lower cauldrons affect your state of mind, your state of mind affects the two lower cauldrons. For example, if your mind is constantly looping with anxious thoughts, you may be prone to gut issues and insomnia, and your relationships may be characterized by mistrust and fear. Conversely, if you keep a healthy perspective on your own thoughts, realizing that they represent just one sliver of reality—or one voice on the microphone—you will enjoy better health in your body and greater peace in your heart.

Most of us are accustomed to placing a lot of importance on our own thoughts. We hear an opinion, suggestion, prediction, or verdict inside our mind, and we immediately take it to be not only true but urgent. For example, your mind might deliver the verdict *This is a disaster!* when you get a flat tire, or opine *That's never going to work* when your partner suggests a new way of dealing with conflict. Yet if there was a scientific way to measure the degree of correlation between our thoughts and reality, most of us would be astounded by how weak this connection is.

Imagine if a friend called you up and said something like this: "I'm doomed! There's no way I'm going to finish this project by Friday, and if I ask for help my boss is going to think I'm incompetent. My only option is to pull all-nighters until it's finished, and if I do that, I'm going to have to miss my sister's birthday party, which is going to do wonders for our relationship."

If you were listening to your friend's thoughts, would you automatically agree that all of these statements were true? I'm going to guess that, on the contrary, you would gently point out all the assumptions your friend was making out of fear ("my boss is going to think I'm incompetent!") and the ways in which he was getting trapped in tunnel vision ("my only option is . . ."). Yet, if these thoughts were running through your own mind, you would probably insist they were 100 percent true.

In the corporate world, there's a phenomenon known as Not Invented Here, in which people tend to resist ideas and processes that did not originate from within their own mind, or at least within their own team, group, or organization. We automatically perceive our own ideas as being particularly credible, while automatically viewing others' ideas as being just the tiniest bit suspect. Overcoming this bias requires humility, but the rewards are great. Once you realize that your surface-level thoughts are mostly just chatter, you can allow them to do their thing in the background, without being ruled by them. And once your flashy, noisy, surface-level thoughts have been consigned to the background, you can listen deeply for the voice of wisdom.

Remember, the upper cauldron is known as the cauldron of *wisdom*—not the cauldron of thought. Wisdom is the deep insight born of experience, and the truth won after careful reflection. It isn't something you can cook up in a hurry, but a flavor that emerges after long and sometimes laborious tending of the self. By learning to distinguish wisdom from thought, you can create the kind of calm and steady conditions within your upper cauldron that will allow you to fulfill your creative and spiritual potential.

▲▽

EXERCISE
Moving Past Opinions

Although it can be tempting to fight your own mind, or rebuke yourself for having unwanted thoughts, it's much more effective to treat yourself with love and respect, no matter what's going on in your head.

The next time you catch your mind forming an opinion based on fear, jealousy, or insecurity, place your hands together with the palms touching, make a gentle bow, and say, "Thank you for sharing your opinion. I'll consider it."

There is no need to fight your mind or feel bad about yourself for having reactions and opinions—this is just what minds do. By bowing to your mind and saying thanks, you create space for that opinion to exist, while buying time for your higher self to emerge and provide you with other possibilities.

Once you have thanked your inner voice for offering its opinion, you can make a gentle request for alternate opinions from your other inner voices. For example, you might say, *What else might be true?* or *Are there other ways of looking at this?* or *I ask that my higher self or Guides provide some insight into this matter.*

Trust that the wisdom you seek is inside you, and don't be alarmed if the first wave of opinions your mind returns aren't the most helpful or productive ones. Keep looking, and you can always find that beautiful grain of truth.

Virtue and the Upper Cauldron

The next crucial task to undertake in preparation for turning your upper cauldron right side up is to firmly establish yourself in virtue. Spiritual practices from shamanism to Zen to yoga have all been known to give serious, long-time practitioners an extra rush of energy—whether that takes the form of increased physical vigor, personal charisma, or remarkable talents in a certain field. This is sometimes true with Celtic shamanism as well. For example, a student of mine who had been practicing for many years began to have intense premonitions which often turned out to be true. She felt that her upper cauldron was receiving information she hadn't been able to access before, and this was both exciting and stressful because it was a huge responsibility for her to take on.

Luckily, this student had always been sincere, humble, and honest in her shamanic undertakings, so she was able to handle this upper cauldron gift with grace and appropriate caution. Thanks to the work she had done with her lower and middle cauldrons, she was able to absorb the extra energy she was receiving without becoming unbalanced or having it negatively affect her work or relationships.

In contrast, if you are not firmly established in the habit of being ethical, truthful, humble, and sincere, this extra energy can lead you down a path of arrogance, greed, and vanity. Just think of leaders who have an undeniable sparkle but mistreat the followers they've attracted, or the healers who may be well qualified but demand exorbitant fees for their services. Even a small boost of spiritual energy can be dangerous if you haven't laid the moral groundwork with which to use it appropriately.

The Celts held honesty, humility, and reverence as their central values—especially when it came to their spiritual practice. They knew from a long tradition that hubris, arrogance, and power-seeking behaviors would always backfire in the end. But the ancient Celts weren't the only ones to emphasize a strong ethical foundation in spiritual practice. The Yoga Sutras of Patanjali speak of the importance of establishing oneself firmly in *sila*, or virtue, before attempting to reach deep meditative states, much less engaging in advanced practices that could result in *siddhis*—spiritual gifts. Christians have the ten commandments and require extra moral commitments from their priests, monks, and nuns. Buddhists are often asked to refrain from lying, stealing, and inappropriate sexual activity, and to abide by a list of moral precepts.

The purpose of establishing oneself in virtue isn't to become a perfect angel, although you may well find yourself becoming calmer, kinder, and more angelic. Establishing yourself in virtue at every level is deeply practical. When your heart and mind are agitated with worry that you will get caught for some less-than-scrupulous action you took, or that you will be exposed for lying, cheating, or taking advantage of others, it's much harder to sink into the deep meditative states where the real inner work gets done. If your ego is running the show, it's much harder to hear the quiet whispers of spirit, and to apply those messages in your daily life.

By taking your cue from the ancient Celts and establishing yourself firmly in the virtues of honesty, humility, and reverence, you can give yourself the best possible chance to fulfill your spiritual potential in a way that makes you kinder, more generous, and a better servant to all forms of life. Let's take a closer look at each of these virtues and how we can apply them in our shamanic practice.

Honesty

Honesty means being truthful and sincere in all your interactions, and not pretending to be someone or something that you are not. It means being clear and factual in your communication, instead of self-aggrandizing or mystifying to impress others; and it means being willing to admit when you don't know the answer or feel uncertain.

One of my students attended a shamanic ritual where participants were invited to create a talisman which they later threw into a bonfire. During the closing circle, other attendees reported experiencing major physical and emotional releases after tossing their talismans into the fire. When it was time for my student to speak, she hesitated. Although she had found the ritual meaningful, she hadn't felt any profound shifts physically or emotionally. Should she speak honestly, or try to come up with a more dramatic description of her experience to match the others? She decided to speak plainly and simply.

Afterward, another attendee came up to thank her for her honesty. "I always feel like I'm failing if I don't have something big and important to report," he said, "but you reminded me that the quiet, everyday experiences are the most important ones." By being honest, she created a space for other participants to show up authentically—and she didn't create a false image she then had to maintain.

Eliminating dishonesty at every level is quite possibly the most important step you can take in establishing virtue. This is because lying to yourself creates a kind of debt that you will become less and less able to repay the bigger the lie becomes. For example, if you claim to have a certain ability, you must then scramble to develop the ability in question before the lie is found out. This kind of indebtedness creates a lot of stress and pressure—whereas if you are always honest about your abilities, you never put yourself in this position.

Lying can also leave you with a sense of disconnection from your life. Hiding your truth from others is a very lonely way to live. There's a reason people speak ruefully of the years they spent "living a lie," whether that's in the context of a relationship, a career, a sexual orientation, or something else. Lying turns us into ghosts, haunting our own lives instead of truly inhabiting them. It takes courage to live from a place of truth, but the rewards are well worth it.

For me, eliminating dishonesty was downright terrifying. What would people think of me if I let my true feelings show? What would *I* think of me if I admitted to being confused, uncertain, or just plain wrong about certain things? How could I survive in today's competitive world if I didn't blur the truth, just like seemingly everybody else? Wouldn't I be putting myself at a great disadvantage?

There are many beautiful Celtic fairy tales about the consequences of lying. One of my favorites tells the story of a young boy who tells fibs. One day, the boy makes the mistake of lying to a wise old woman who sees right through his deceit. This wise woman casts a spell on the boy. Now, every time he tells a lie, a toad, bat, rat, or some other creature appears and begins to follow him around. At first, the boy finds this funny, but it's not long before he is surrounded by a menagerie of croaking, scuttling, rasping sidekicks who follow him wherever he goes, causing havoc in his life.

The boy goes to the wise woman and begs for help, but the old woman tells him that the only way to break the spell is to confess to his lies and apologize to the people he has deceived. I'm sure you can guess what happens next—the boy changes his ways and goes on to live an honest life.

I love the way this story uses a swarm of toads, bats, and other creatures as a metaphor for the complications that can proliferate when we lie to ourselves or others. Lying means keeping up with an elaborate set of alternate facts—or in some cases, several sets of alternate facts—and this takes a lot of energy. When we show up as who we really are and say what we mean, we can free ourselves from this unwelcome labor and move through the world unburdened and at peace.

Humility

Although in modern times people sometimes mistake humility with a lack of confidence or low self-esteem, being humble really means keeping an accurate perspective on who and what you are. Every life is precious, from the smallest insect to the tallest tree, the most "average" person to the most celebrated individual in human history. Although it is good to recognize and honor the sacredness of your own life, humility is the act of bowing to everyone you meet, recognizing that their life is likewise precious and sacred. It's remembering that no matter how "advanced" you become—in your spiritual practice, your artistic pursuits, your career, or any other calling—you still have much to learn from the people around you, as well as from the nonhuman world. When you are truly humble, you can admit your shortcomings and actively work to improve, instead of wallowing in your real or perceived flaws.

Many of us use pride or even arrogance as a shield against buried feelings of shame and worthlessness. We believe that who and what we really are isn't enough, so our next best option is to create a confident, know-it-all self who *is* enough. But as soon as we build that false self, we immediately become afraid that someone will see through it. We learn to hide our mistakes and deny our flaws, instead of using them as opportunities to grow our vulnerability. We give ourselves the impossible task of being superior, then exhaust ourselves in trying to carry it out.

What a relief it is to shed the burden of trying to be smarter, faster, and better than everyone else, and embrace the virtue of humility. This is not to say that we shouldn't strive for excellence—but we can do so slowly and patiently, without rushing to make too much of ourselves overnight. Not only does the virtue of humility keep us safe when we engage in spiritual practice, but it reminds us that we are already perfect exactly as we are—nothing can increase or diminish the value of our lives here on earth.

Myths and fairy tales from around the world contrast the perils of vanity with the riches of humility. Just think of the classic tortoise and hare story. I've seen versions of this in my own work, as students who work quietly and humbly frequently surpass their louder, flashier peers in no time. In the words of Ernest Hemingway, "There is nothing noble in being superior to your fellow man; true nobility is being superior to your former self."

Reverence

In today's culture there is, for the most part, a lack of reverence for the natural and unseen worlds. Most of us are certainly never told that the forest is full of spirits who should be respected, that the birds and spiders are relatives we should honor, or that it is sometimes appropriate to be silent instead of speaking. Instead, we are taught that nature is something to tromp through and take photos of rather than a rich and complex realm teeming with other forms of consciousness. Like children playing video games during a funeral, we move through life oblivious to its gravity and sacredness—and this lack of reverence diminishes not only the natural world, but ourselves. By restoring our connection to reverence, we restore our own humanity.

Like many shamanic peoples around the world, the Celts embodied reverence in all of their interactions with the sacred. They likely performed ablutions, or cleansing rituals, before partaking in certain ceremonies, and took care to handle sacred objects with respect. They would not have rushed through rituals or performed them casually, but brought attention and focus to every word and movement. When passing by sacred places such as lakes or caves, they would not speak in loud voices, but would pause and show those places proper respect, often by leaving an offering.

Reverence opens the heart, imbuing us with a sense of awe and gratitude for the great mystery of life. Cultivating reverence puts you in closer touch with nature, and strengthens your relationship with the divine. Reverence and humility go hand in hand; it's impossible to be both arrogant and reverent at the same time, since being reverent means acknowledging the existence of forces greater than yourself. It is also nearly impossible to be dishonest when you are in a state of reverence. With this in mind, cultivating reverence makes it much easier to develop the other virtues.

One of my favorite ways to show reverence is by taking care with my opening and closing rituals when I take a shamanic journey or conduct a ritual. By slowly and mindfully lighting candles, saining, and otherwise preparing my space, and taking care in how I handle my drum and ritual objects, I remind myself that I am interfacing with the divine. I remember that the reverence I express in my shamanic work is directly correlated to the quality of the insights I receive.

EXERCISE
Cultivating Reverence

Like gratitude, reverence is a mental attitude you can choose to cultivate, whether or not you were raised in a culture that prizes it. And like gratitude, scientists have found that experiences of awe and reverence come with health benefits ranging from increased happiness to increased altruism toward others. When we experience the sacred in the world around us, we become kinder, more generous, and more content. To cultivate awe and reverence in your life, try to do one of the following for a few minutes every day:

- Walk through a garden, looking at flowers, insects, and tree bark through a loupe or magnifying glass. Seeing these things up close will get you out of your habitual way of seeing and is sure to inspire awe.

- In the springtime, try to find a bird's nest with chicks inside. (You can often do this by watching parents fly back to the nest with food in their beaks.) Watch the parent birds feeding their young. If you're lucky, you might get to see those baby birds grow up and become adults themselves—a true miracle of nature.

- Go to a lake, river, or other body of water just before sunrise. Watch and listen as the first light hits the water. Listen to the birds, watch the animals through the reeds, and witness a new day taking shape.

- Sit on your front steps, porch, or balcony at night and watch the moon rise.

- Watch rain or snow falling.

- Lie in a grassy place and watch the clouds float by.

By engaging in these practices for even a few minutes, you quickly realize that there is no end to beauty and wonder—you just need to slow down enough to let it in. Training your mind to pay worshipful attention to the mysteries of nature is a recipe for lasting happiness and inner peace.

▲▼

EXERCISE
Committing to the Three Virtues

Among Buddhists, there is an initiation called *jukai* in which students make a formal commitment to the five precepts: refraining from lying, killing, stealing, sexual misconduct, and ingesting intoxicating substances (or, to frame it in positive terms, agreeing to be honest, ethical, humble, and discerning.) A jukai ceremony is a happy occasion on which participants bathe and dress in clean clothes, make vows in the presence of their community, and sometimes receive special garments or even dharma names from their teachers. Often, the participants have spent months studying the precepts in depth and pondering what these virtues mean in their daily lives.

Modern Celtic shamans sometimes carry out similar ceremonies to affirm and celebrate our commitment to ethical spiritual practice. You can do this in community, with the presence and support of other shamans, or in private, with nature as your witness.

To begin, spend some time contemplating each of the three virtues. Where can you deepen your honesty? Your humility? Your reverence? How have your lapses from these virtues caused trouble for you in the past, and what do you hope to gain by committing to them on a deep level? Use your journal to explore these questions in depth. If you are in touch with a shamanic community or even one sincere friend, take some time to discuss them together.

Next, take a ritual bath. This can take the form of a candlelit bath in your home, a dip in a lake or river, or any other ritual that feels cleansing to you. As you bathe, recall your intention to live with virtue. You may also take this time to reflect with wise remorse on the times when you have neglected to live with virtue.

After you have bathed, sit with your drum or in quiet meditation. Allow yourself to feel that other shamans all over the world are supporting you in your decision to live with virtue. If you are working with any Guides or spirit helpers, you can call on them for assistance in living a life of virtue.

Next, give thanks to any friends or teachers who have modeled virtue for you in the past. You might call these people to mind one by one, inwardly sending them gratitude for the ways their virtue has touched your life.

To complete the ceremony, make a spoken invocation in which you affirm your commitment to virtue. For example, "May I be humble, sincere, and ethical in all my undertakings, for the benefit of all beings."

Allow yourself to feel the purity and brightness of your upper cauldron when you commit to an ethical life.

▲▼▲

Preparing the Upper Cauldron to Receive

There is a famous Zen story about a student, Scholar Tokusan, who approaches a Zen master named Ryutan, asking for his wisdom. Ryutan pours some tea for Tokusan, but he doesn't stop pouring when the teacup is full. "Stop!" says Tokusan. "It's overflowing." Ryu-tan replies, "You are just like this cup. You come to me asking for wisdom, but you are already full of ideas and opinions of your own. If you really want me to teach you, you first need to empty your cup."

The same is true of the upper cauldron. When we are filled with ideas, opinions, pride, and over-confidence, there's little room for divine wisdom to appear. But when we empty ourselves—by practic-ing virtue, and holding our own thoughts with skep-ticism—we create a beautiful vessel which is ready to be filled with the inspiration of the gods. Unlike the emptiness of a drained lower cauldron, an empty upper cauldron is wonderful and desirable, because it means we are ready to receive.

Chapter 8

Upper Cauldron Work for Personal Transformation

Human beings have come up with countless names for the experience of transcending everyday consciousness and touching the divine. The yogis of India speak of a kundalini awakening in which energy rushes up the spine and out through the crown of the head; Zen practitioners speak of flashes of eternity glimpsed in *kensho*; Sufis experience *wajad*, or religious ecstasy. In the West, scientists have called this experience a flow state, a peak experience, or being "in the zone." Shamans, too, experience these spiritual highs—moments when divine inspiration rushes in, and things just seem to, well, make sense.

In Celtic shamanism, these experiences are understood to happen when the upper cauldron turns right side up—no matter how briefly. You might be meditating with your drum, carrying out a ritual, or making an offering in nature when a deep sense of peace descends upon you and you feel a sense of oneness with all of creation. For hours, days, or even months afterward, you might find that your work flows more easily, songs and stories come to you seemingly out of nowhere, and your life seems charged with mystical coincidences you can't quite explain. When you experience an upper cauldron righting, you will remember it for the rest of your life.

I will never forget my first experience of an upper cauldron opening. I was sitting in the Scottish hill country with my drum, near some standing stones, in the early morning. The grass was sparkly with dew. I could feel the energy of the standing stones nearby, eternal and wise. In the previous months, I'd been doing a lot of work with my lower and middle cauldrons, cultivating my energy and slowly unraveling the old fears that were holding me back. On the morning in question, I'd brought an offering of dried rose petals and rosemary sprigs to leave at the base of the standing stones, and asked my spirit guides to help me find the wisdom I needed to navigate the challenges in my life.

As I drummed, I found myself sinking into a deep meditative state. The sun was rising on the hillside, and the blades of grass turned gold and emerald in the light. Suddenly, I began to sing—a simple chant that seemed to contain both sorrow and joy, and felt timeless in its circularity. I'm not sure where the song came from or to whom it belonged—certainly, I had no sense that "I" was composing it. On the contrary, it felt like the song was coming through me. The notes and sounds felt deeply healing as I sang them again and again, my drum keeping time in the background.

Everything around me felt imbued with beauty—not only the shining grass and the drops of dew, but even the highway snaking in the distance, the cars strung one after another like beads on a necklace. I felt a profound sense of love and connection for everyone and everything, including myself. Although I didn't think to articulate it at the time, I felt that all three of my cauldrons were upright and working in harmony, their energy circulating freely within my body, filling me with this wonderful sense of divinity and grace.

When I left the hillside that day, I knew that I had received a great gift. In the flood of reverence and connection I experienced, all the things I was used to thinking of as "problems" didn't look like problems at all. I realized my life was perfect exactly the way it was, and all the beauty I needed was already inside me and all around me. At the same time, I knew that what I'd experienced wasn't particular and unique to me, but had been shared by countless others over the course of human history. Just knowing that I could access this higher state of being made me feel much calmer, more centered, and at ease in my day-to-day life.

▲▼

EXERCISE
Omen Walks

Journeying with a drum is not the only way to tap into a sense of mystical oneness. Omen walking is the practice of taking a walk in nature or in an urban area with the intention of receiving signs and messages related to a specific question you have about your life. It's a way to "turn up" your ordinary connection to intuition, inner knowing, and the helping spirits of the land where you live.

Omen walking can help you shift out of your regular patterns of thinking and open yourself to less-common ways of receiving information. To start, identify your intention for the omen walk. Are you asking for clarity, actionable advice, healing, or information? Write down your intention on a piece of paper and place it in your pocket, purse, or bag.

Next, sain yourself, burn a stick of incense, or conduct any other small ritual signifying your openness to receiving divine wisdom.

When you are ready to begin your omen walk, simply relax and enjoy your surroundings. As you walk, allow answers to come to you in the form of signs, stirrings, and inner knowings. Omen walks work best if you don't try too hard, but wait for the signs or omens to come to you.

My most treasured omen walk was in the middle of the city of Edinburgh. I'd been struggling to make a decision that would affect my family and I asked for guidance on what I should focus on as I considered my options. As I walked through the Old Town, I saw three lorries in ten minutes that all had the word Eve emblazoned in big, bold letters on the side. I had my answer: focus on my daughter and her needs. After this omen walk, my decision was easy.

Whenever you go on an omen walk, it is important to honor the wisdom and guidance you are given. For example, if you receive signs or guidance about specific actions to take, do your best to put those into practice. I also like to give thanks and offerings after an omen walk, and sain myself a second time when I get home.

Celtic Shamanism and the Right Brain

If you've done any reading about neuroscience, you probably already know that the human brain has two hemispheres with distinctly different ways of processing information. The left brain is logical and analytical. It is constantly making up stories and theories to explain why things happen, and finds it very difficult to give up this habit even in the face of evidence that its theories are useless or incorrect. It is very skilled at making narratives, teasing out cause and effect, and narrowing in on specific details. The left brain also loves to insist on finding solutions based on the information it already has instead of considering new information.

The right brain, in contrast, is intuitive, creative, and much more open to new ideas. When you are operating from your right brain, you see reality in all its marvelous complexity, and not in terms of the comparatively narrow and limited story your left brain is making up about things. The right brain is where we experience flashes of insight, deep inner knowings, and creative visions. Artists spend a lot of time in their right brains, staring into space and waiting for the right word, sound, or color to come to them. When I spontaneously began to sing on the hillside, that was a function of my right brain.

Some researchers believe that human beings used to be right-brain dominant and evolved to become left-brain dominant as a result of our sophisticated use of language and technology. Celts and other ancient peoples probably experienced their own consciousness differently than people do today, and this is no surprise—our consciousness is a reflection of our environment, after all. As modern shamans, we sometimes need a little help to access our right brains, especially if our jobs require us to spend many hours a day in our logical left brains. Omen walking is one way to shift into our right brains; shamanic drumming is another.

When we drum at a steady rate of four to seven beats per second for fifteen minutes or so, our brains naturally begin to shift into a theta-wave state, which is associated with deep relaxation, hypnosis, and dreaming. This theta-wave state allows our conscious mind to let go, making way for the wisdom of the subconscious to bubble up in myriad beautiful ways. If your upper cauldron is dominated by linear left-brain thinking, spending more time with your drum or in other meditative practices can help you develop your intuitive, creative, divinely inspired right brain—which has been there all along but can sometimes need a little encouragement to come forth.

Whenever I feel that my upper cauldron is getting cluttered with too much linear thinking, planning, and worrying, I make sure to spend more time with my drum. This simple practice never fails to shift me back toward my right brain, in which worries more or less cease to exist, and life seems to be made all of one piece, instead of a hopeless jumble of parts. If you are preparing for a creative undertaking such as writing a poem or song, working on a painting, or even solving a mechanical, relational, or work-related problem, drumming for fifteen minutes can balance your upper cauldron, letting you access the full range of its gifts.

Invocation

The ancient Celts believed that creative expressions such as poetry and song were not the individual poet or musician's own invention, but a gift from the gods. When the upper cauldron is right side up, it becomes a chalice into which the gods can pour their own divine inspiration; the individual artist or poet is merely a vessel to receive it. Many contemporary artists echo this sentiment when they say that their ideas "just came to them" or that they feel like they channeled their work rather than consciously creating it.

One of the most potent forms of creative expression practiced by both ancient and contemporary Celtic shamans is the art of invocation—spontaneous, performative, often-poetic speech that causes a shift in the speaker and listeners' consciousness and sometimes in reality itself. In the secular, modern world it is still common to hear invocations at weddings, when the officiant and other speakers call in the qualities of love and commitment they wish to bestow upon the couple getting married. You might also find yourself using invocation during highly emotional moments, such as when a friend is moving away and you deliver an unexpected oration about all the blessings you wish for them in their new home.

In Celtic shamanism, we use the art of invocation for many purposes: to open and close sacred space before and after going on a journey or conducting a ritual; to invoke the qualities of certain gods, spirits, or natural elements during a ceremony or ritual; to sain ourselves or a space; and while making offerings. When we make invocations, we allow the divine to speak through us, merging ourselves with a form of inspiration that is just a bit greater than what we could normally access on our own.

How does invocation differ from everyday speech—or, for that matter, from a formal speech prepared in advance? The first piece is simply intention. When we make an invocation, our intention is to bridge the gap between the ordinary and the divine. We are conscious of our words holding a kind of energetic charge, and this creates a paradox: on the one hand, we want to choose our words carefully; on the other hand, we want to tip our cauldron right side up and let divine inspiration flow into it spontaneously. This combination of taking great care *and* letting go is reminiscent of the way that great musicians describe their best performances onstage.

Like great musicians, we can prepare ourselves to enter this special state with practice. Let's say you are preparing for a ritual in which you wish to invoke the wisdom of the bard Taliesin to guide you through a difficult time. In advance of this ritual, you may spend a little time each day considering Taliesin's qualities and why you wish to summon these qualities to yourself. You might write down a few sentences of invocation for practice, even as you keep in mind that a written speech and a spoken invocation are two different things. You might practice speaking these sentences out loud, feeling the rise and fall of your voice and listening to the sounds of the words.

In the modern world, many of us struggle with invocation. We feel self-conscious and awkward, or we worry that we aren't "authorized" to speak in a sacred way. When I began my spiritual journey, I felt uneasy and disconnected from my confident voice. Although I knew the importance of invocation, I struggled to come up with words on the spot. Instead, I composed them in advance of my journeys and rituals. The first time I wrote my own invocation, it seemed so precious to me that I printed and laminated it! This makes me laugh now, as I've since come to learn the importance of spontaneous invocation in keeping your connection to the divine fresh and meaningful.

As my confidence increased, I discovered the power of speaking freely instead of preparing my words in advance. When I let go of control and allowed my words to come from a place of authenticity, they had a greater impact on my spiritual practice. The words that came from my heart were filled with love, gratitude, and intention, and they helped me to connect with the divine in a deeper way.

Here is an example of an opening invocation I might use as part of a sacred space–setting ritual:

I call on, acknowledge, and thank the sky above, the sea all around, and the earth below; the loving ancestors, and my spiritual guides. I feel your divine presence and ask that you hold me in a safe, sacred temple of light, only available for experiences that are for my best and highest good. My intention for this ritual is [X], and I am open to exactly what is right for me today. I hold no attachment to the outcome and surrender myself to the loving arms of the divine. This space is open.

At certain times, you might also choose to invoke the qualities of a certain being, archetype, power animal, or element of nature. If you are drawn to the Celtic pantheon, these might include Lugh, Brid, the Morrigan, Cerridwen, or the Dagda; however, there is no need to limit yourself to Celtic figures. If you are drawn to figures from other traditions, or to specific beings or deities you have encountered in the course of shamanic journeying, you can invoke their qualities too. You might also invoke the steadiness of an oak tree, the infinite nature of running water, or the beauty of the rising moon, connecting with them with reverence and drawing their qualities into your own being.

▲▼

EXERCISE
Invocation

The next time you find yourself in need of strength, wisdom, confidence, kindness, or any other positive energy, try invoking a deity, archetype, or element of nature that represents that quality to you.

To begin, choose the god, goddess, spirit being, or natural element you wish to invoke.

Open your space by lighting a candle. Breathing mindfully, see yourself held in a sacred, healing temple of light. Let that vision grow as you feel your Guides or ancestors gather around you.

Picking up your drum, begin to play at a slow, steady pace. As you drum, meditate on all aspects of this being: What do they look like? What do they sound like? How would they act in your situation?

Next, call out to this being using your voice. For example, you might say, "I call on the spirit of the Morrigan. Please fill me with your courage and ferocity as I undertake this task."

As you continue to drum, imagine that this deity or being has heard you and agreed to lend you the qualities you are requesting. Feel yourself becoming stronger, wiser, kinder, or filled with whichever other quality you are invoking.

Continue to drum until you feel that these qualities have become well-established inside yourself.

When you feel complete, call out again, thanking the being in question for granting you their gifts. Allow your drumming to slowly come to a halt. Extinguish your candle and state that your space is closed.

Offerings and the Upper Cauldron

When you invoke the qualities of a certain deity, power animal, natural feature, or ancestor, you can deepen the connection by making an offering. In Celtic shamanism, there are two types of offerings: gratitude offerings and votive offerings. Gratitude offerings are those we give as a form of thanks and praise. For example, you might gather wildflowers to offer at a waterfall, or make an offering of incense to a deity who inspires you. Votive offerings are those we give when we are requesting insight or healing. Both types of offerings are thought to have been common among the ancient Celts, and contemporary shamans frequently practice both as well.

Giving offerings is a way of acknowledging that your gifts do not belong to you—they were granted to you by life itself, and they will return to the vast and infinite pool of life someday. With this in mind, making an offering helps us to stay humble, and stay out of the trap of believing that we have "earned" our gifts or that we possess them in some way. Leaving offerings reminds us that life is a constant flow. Energy is always passing through us in one form or another, nourishing us and allowing us to nourish others in turn.

For example, when you have a brilliant idea, it's never really "yours," but builds on the thinking and pondering of millions of humans who came before you. When you succeed at a project or task, that success belongs to everyone who taught you and supported you, no matter how distant in the past that teaching and support may be. There is no such thing as individual genius, no matter what our story-making left brains tell us—we are all interconnected so densely that some spiritual teachers say it's an illusion to talk about a separate "I" at all.

As you leave offerings, you can ask nature, your higher self, or your spirit guides for advice on how to best use your gifts. Seeing as your gifts don't really belong to you, how can you use them to benefit as many people and other organisms as possible? Asking this question is a beautiful practice and will ensure that your upper cauldron work remains grounded in benevolence.

Offerings don't have to take the form of material objects. You can also make an offering of your time and labor—for example, volunteering at a homeless shelter or taking part in a social justice demonstration. At the subtlest level, you can even make an offering of your own attention moment to moment, no matter where you are or what you are doing. Life wants to be noticed, admired, and appreciated; when you pay attention to the curling edges of a table cloth blowing in the wind, or to the sound of your neighbor practicing violin, you are making a very deep kind of offering indeed.

EXERCISE
Ancestor Altars

A beautiful way to incorporate offerings into your life is by creating an altar for your ancestors. Shamanic peoples the world over have long believed that we do not journey through this lifetime alone, but are supported and protected by the ones who came before us. The spirits of our ancestors live on in our own blood, and under ideal circumstances we can feel strengthened and inspired by this connection. Paying homage to your ancestors reminds you that you are just one link in a long chain of existence: your joys and sorrows do not belong solely to you, but to your whole family tree, in more complex and subtle ways than you may ever understand. Tending an ancestral altar can give you a sense of purpose and help you feel less alone.

To begin, identify the ancestors you wish to honor. If you do not resonate with any of your biological ancestors, or have no information about them, it's perfectly fine to honor ancestors from outside your family tree, as well as any spiritual, cultural, or creative lineages to which you belong.

Next, gather photographs or objects representing these ancestors.

In the mornings, take some time to connect to the energy of these ancestors. You can reflect on the struggles they overcame, express gratitude for the sacrifices they made, and ask for their help and guidance in overcoming your own challenges.

On special days, such as death anniversaries or birthdays, consider making an offering to a specific ancestor by burning a candle or incense and leaving a gift of food.

Whether or not you have children, take some time to reflect on what it would mean for you to someday become a wise and loving ancestor. How would you like people to think of you after you die? Which qualities would you like people to reflect on when they place your portrait on their own ancestral altar? What can you do to embody those qualities in your life today?

Helping Others with Shamanism

As your three cauldrons come into balance, you may find that you have greater inner resources to help the people around you. For example, you may become a better listener, and have a deeper capacity to hear and empathize with people's pain. People may seek you out as a confidante or even as a healer—or you may be tempted to offer shamanic services to others, by going on journeys to seek answers for them, leading them through healing rituals, or using your spiritual gifts to give them insight or advice.

A student of mine found himself in exactly this situation. Thanks to his work with shamanism, he had developed a quality of kindness and empathy that drew people in. Total strangers would approach him to tell him their life stories and ask for advice. Most of the time, he just listened, and that seemed to be enough. But one time, a close friend of his convinced him to conduct a healing ritual on her behalf. Even though he felt uncertain about it, his friend was in so much distress he didn't feel like he could refuse her.

He conducted a simple ritual with the goal of giving her relief from the nightmares and insomnia which had been plaguing her. As part of this ritual, he visualized his friend sleeping soundly, surrounded by safe, loving energy. Although the ritual itself was positive, benevolent, and harmless, his friend continued to have nightmares and insomnia—only now, she felt even more distressed because the ritual hadn't "fixed" her like she'd hoped. She spiraled into a deep depression, and my student felt responsible. Even though he hadn't done anything wrong, he was left with feelings of guilt and confusion he wasn't sure how to handle. He decided not to offer shamanic services to others until he'd received training on how to navigate this kind of situation.

Although it's understandable that you may want to use your gifts to alleviate another person's suffering, the safest way to do this is through everyday acts of kindness, generosity, and decency, not by attempting to seek answers for others or offering shamanic healing services before you're truly ready. When you offer healing services to another, you entangle your-self with that person energetically—often to a greater degree than you expected or intended. Skilled sha-mans know how to navigate this kind of entangle-ment safely and cleanly, but beginners often find themselves in over their heads. In contrast, simple kindness and decency are underrated, and far safer for all parties involved.

If you do find yourself drawn to using your shamanic gifts to heal others, check in with your-self to make sure that all three of your cauldrons are in a good position to do so. Is your lower cauldron upright, full, and able to support you in supporting someone else? Is your middle cauldron holding good boundaries with this person? Are you coming from a place of love, stability, and humility? Is there a sense of obligation, or a hint of ambition or pride? Is your upper cauldron clear and untroubled? Do all three of your "minds" agree that you can offer your energy to this person safely and without becoming drained or overly entangled?

If the answer is yes, ask yourself if you can help this person without entering into a healer-client relationship with them. Can you simply listen with kindness? Can you hold in your heart the intention that they be happy, healthy, and at peace? There is no need to jump into the deep end with elaborate rituals and journeys, or even to identify yourself as a shaman or healer. Simply seeing a person in light is powerful medicine in its own right, and by working slowly and carefully with this medicine, you can develop your healing gifts in a safe and balanced way. You can also share this book with others so they can explore their own shamanic work, and I encourage you to check out our community of shamans at the Centre for Shamanism. There are people at all stages of their shamanic journey working together to find solutions to problems, and simply hearing about others' struggles and what's worked for them could be helpful too.

▲▼

EXERCISE
Three Cauldrons Breathwork

Sometimes, working with others can leave you feeling tired and unsettled. This meditation helps bring your three cauldrons into balance, allowing your energy to flow harmoniously between them.

To begin, visualize your lower cauldron sitting at the level of your belly. Breathe into this space, allowing your belly to completely fill with air and then deflate again. As you do so, feel yourself filling your lower cauldron with the grounding energy of the earth.

Next, visualize your middle cauldron sitting at the level of your heart. Breathe into your heart, feeling it expand with love and compassion. At the same time, maintain awareness of your lower cauldron supporting your heart from below. Feel your middle cauldron filling with expansive energy of the ocean.

Then visualize your upper cauldron sitting at the level of your head. Breathe into the space between your eyes—also known as your pineal gland or your third eye—feeling yourself opening to divine inspiration. Maintain awareness of your lower and middle cauldrons supporting your upper cauldron from below. Feel your upper cauldron filling with the wide-open wisdom of the sky.

Now, feel the energy circulating between all three cauldrons in a constant flow—rising up from your lower cauldron, passing through your middle and upper cauldrons, and cascading down again like a waterfall. Feel your mental, emotional, and physical bodies becoming integrated and harmonious.

Complete this practice by putting your hands together in a posture of gratitude and giving thanks to the earth that sustains you.

Embracing Intuition

As you work with your upper cauldron, you will find that your intuition becomes clearer. Intuition can manifest as physical sensations, bodily reflexes, thoughts, or silent knowings. For example, you may feel unexpectedly drawn to starting a conversation with the person sitting next to you on an airplane, whose life turns out to be connected to yours in ways you couldn't have predicted; or you may have a "random" instinct to take a different route home from work one day, only to find out later that you avoided an accident.

Intuition is a mysterious intelligence whose origins you can't always explain but whose gifts can transform you. Shamans the world over have long been associated with this mysterious intelligence, which emerges after years of steady cultivation. Yet intuition doesn't just work from the inside out; it works from the outside in. For example, one shaman I know has the uncanny ability to be in the right place at the right time. On the one hand, her strong inner knowing guides her to these places; at the same time, wherever she is *becomes* the right place thanks to her state of openness. By developing your intuition, you can expand the range of what feels right and meaningful to you.

Often, this shift toward intuition is accompanied by a deepening sense of trust in life. When your upper cauldron is functioning in harmony with the two lower ones, you realize that you don't need to think or plan so much, because you know that you can handle whatever arises, at the moment it arises. Not only can you trust yourself to respond gracefully and appropriately to any situation, but you know that you are part of a vast and beautiful web of life which is supporting you at every moment of every day. You can place one foot in front of the other, allowing the path to appear, trusting that no matter how thick the mist becomes, there is something wonderful waiting for you on the other side.

Seeing Through the Eyes of Love

One summer evening not too long ago, I sat down with my drum and embarked on a solitary journey. Although I'd had a hectic day, it didn't take long for the beat of my drum to calm my mind and send me deep into a trance state. I soon drifted into a daydream in which I saw myself walking through a forest of towering oak trees, their leaves whispering in the wind. After a while, I came upon a large clearing with a turquoise blanket in its center. I understood that I was to lie on the blanket and gaze up at the crowns of the trees.

As soon as I did so, my entire life began to play out before my eyes, beginning with my birth and continuing all the way up to that very day. I saw my parents, my brothers and sisters, my school friends, and my teachers. No matter what role these people had played in my life on a surface level, I now experienced every one of them as beings of divine love, who had been helping me and teaching me all along. As the events of my life unspooled before my eyes, I felt only joy. I realized that I had been deeply loved throughout every one of these phases, whether or not I knew it at the time—I had been surrounded by divine love since the moment I'd been born.

When your three cauldrons come into balance, it's like focusing a camera lens: suddenly, you can see clearly what you couldn't see before. Instead of being distracted by surface-level stories about the ways you've been hurt, traumatized, and wronged, you begin to see directly to the heart of life—and the heart of life is nothing less than love. Supported by the earthly nature of your lower cauldron, the expansive nature of your middle cauldron, and the celestial nature of your upper cauldron, life starts to reveal its perfection in countless ways.

The most important thing I've learned from practicing Celtic shamanism is that there is no such thing as failure. Our deepest wounds and most difficult emotions are only energy waiting to be transformed into gifts by the loving fire of our inner cauldrons. No matter how badly you've been hurt, or how badly you may have hurt others, you can transform your sorrow, guilt, or anger by slowly and patiently working with your three cauldrons, ensuring that this energy can be put in the service of good.

How do you know if your three cauldrons are coming into balance? It starts with a sense of deep inner wellness. Physically, it can manifest as a sense of serenity, strength, and good health. Emotionally, it can appear as a sense of calm confidence, equilibrium, gratitude, and unflappability. Spiritually, it shows up as the feeling that you are connected to something greater than yourself, and that even when you don't know all the answers, things are still okay. When your three cauldrons are in balance, you will find yourself becoming less reactive, less anxious, and less concerned with the specific ups and downs of life—because you realize that you *are* life.

You *are* the whispering of the oak leaves and the beating of the drum, the fire that crackles beneath the cauldron and the stew that is cooking within it. You are wisdom, strength, kindness, and courage; you are song, poetry, painting, and dance. There is no separation between you and the qualities you wish to possess; you are connected to the web of life in all ways, at all times. Giving and receiving, arising and passing, waking and dormant, life is a constant cycle of transformation, and by merging yourself with that process you need never feel lost, hopeless, or alone.

I hope that this book has given you the tools you need to establish your own connection with the divine, in whatever form that takes for you. By deeply exploring our inner worlds—and establishing reverent and beneficial relationships with the natural world—we honor the sacredness of our lives and the lives of everyone around us. Contemporary Celtic shamanism has the power to reanimate the earth, restore sacred bonds of community, and improve the health and happiness of all those who practice it. My sincere wish is that you enjoy these benefits, and spread them to your neighbors, family, and friends—both human and nonhuman.

May the wisdom of the Celts inspire and guide you, the sacred spirits of the land and water embrace and protect you, and the transformative power of the cauldron and the drum support you every day of your life.

Acknowledgments

Thanks to my husband, Scott, for your unwavering support, keen observations, and willingness to delve into the crunchy details—this book is improved by your thoughtful input.

To David, my business partner and brother—I couldn't do this without your sacrifice, support, and extensive skills in copywriting, web design, software, and more. You are the backbone of our operation, and the only one who can reliably interpret my bubbles.

To Eve and Mirren, my favorite adventure buddies, and life's greatest teachers—otherwise known as my kids. Who knew parenting could be this much fun? (Don't answer that.)

To my office buddy, Wendy, I must thank you not only for putting up with my chatter as I brainstormed for this book but also for your many valuable suggestions and insights.

To the quiet superheroes Josh, Scott, and Wendy, who manage the kids and household tasks while I write, thanks for taking the pressure off. And Josh, thank you for helping with the research for the book.

Thank you, Randy, for finding me, welcoming me into your publishing family, and willingly lending your expertise, good judgment, and time to this book. To Hilary, my editor, thanks for really understanding me and my goals, and making me feel supported and safe in this unfamiliar process. To Grace and Susie, thank you for your time and keen eyes! And to HeatherAsh, thanks for taking time from your busy life to write a beautiful foreword to this book.

A few other vital people in my life who helped me with the real-life research shared in this book include Jayne, my sister, whose conversations open many doors of understanding; Kenny, my best friend and excellent listener of ideas; Isaac, my honorary brother and consistent helping hand in awkward moments; and Jayne and Maria for turning up just when I was losing faith.

To Judith and Judy, who keep me organized and afloat—it's not easy for me to effectively manage my ADHD, but you guys make it simpler and far less stressful. Thanks also to my Gaelic friends Fergus, Morag, and Mark, who help me explore our native language.

To Sam McLaren, the Mary Anning of British indigenous wisdom, thank you for your patience as you answered my many questions, for your dedication to your path, and for saving the rest of us the burden of academic research. I acknowledge there may be academic errors (which are mine and mine alone)— I'll endeavor to update in future editions! And to my original teacher, Carol Day, your ethical magic permeates everything I do both in teaching and in life.

To the Centre for Shamanism community, you guys are as much a part of this book as my Guides—thank you for trusting me with your souls.

To Mum and Dad, who taught me to find magic in the world against all odds, like finding a matching sock on laundry day.

And finally, to my spiritual team, my ancestors, and to the spirits of the land. I'm honoured to be a vessel through which *imbas* can flow.

Resources

The Centre for Shamanism

You can connect with Rhonda at the Centre for Shamanism, of which she is the founder. The Centre for Shamanism has many resources available for those who wish to walk the path of Celtic shamanism, including a free online community, drumming tracks, and how-to guides. Visit the Centre for Shamanism at centreforshamanism.com.

The Cauldron of Poesy

To read the author's preferred translation of Amergin Glúingel's *The Cauldron of Poesy*, visit www.seanet.com/~inisglas/henrycauldronpoesy.pdf.

Further Reading

Beith, Mary. *Healing Threads: Traditional Medicines of the Islands and Highlands.* Edinburgh, Scotland: Birlinn Limited, 2018.

Carmichael, Alexander. *Carmina Gadelica: Hymns and Incantations*. Edinburgh, Scotland: Floris Books, 1992.

Green, Miranda. *Animals in Celtic Life and Myth*. Oxfordshire, England: Routledge, 1998.

MacLeod, Sharon Paice. *Celtic Myth and Religion: A Study of Traditional Belief, with Newly Translated Prayers, Poems, and Songs*. Jefferson, NC: MacFarland & Company, 2011.

Thompson, Francis. *The Supernatural Highlands*. Edinburgh, Scotland: Luath Press Limited, 1997.

Wilby, Emma. *Cunning Folk and Familiar Spirits: Shamanistic Visionary Traditions in Early Modern British Witchcraft and Magic*. Liverpool, England: Liverpool University Press, 2006.

About the Author

Rhonda McCrimmon is a Celtic shaman committed to creating shamanic pathways for those who have been disconnected from their animist lineage and heritage. Walking a shamanic path for over a decade, Rhonda follows her calling with single-minded determination, making shamanic practices accessible for all within an ethical, loving spiritual tribe.

Also from Hierophant Publishing

THE
MEDICINE
BAG

SHAMANIC RITUALS &
CEREMONIES FOR PERSONAL
TRANSFORMATION

DON JOSE RUIZ

New York Times bestselling co-author of
The Fifth Agreement

Available wherever books are sold.

San Antonio, TX
www.hierophantpublishing.com